"This lucid and entirely jargon-free guide to *Paradise Lost* will help any reader of the poem to find their feet, and to understand what makes it the best poem in the English language. Hopkins has one, and only one, resemblance to Milton's Satan, which is that he can make intricate seem straight."

Colin Burrow, Oxford University

"Where most Miltonists use *Paradise Lost* as a quarry for an investigation of the theological and political ideas of the period, Hopkins' book restores the poem to where it properly belongs, the sphere of literature. It treats *Paradise Lost* as a great poem, indeed one of the greatest ever written, and shows what that claim means in its beautiful choice of quotations and illuminating commentary upon them, demonstrating the work's imaginative reach, human interest, and supremely bold and varied verbal artistry. This is the best introduction to *Paradise Lost* there is, suitable for the intelligent sixth-former or undergraduate, or the enquiring general reader outside the academy – or indeed anyone who cares about poetry. It is also a joy to read, indeed a real page-turner – and of how many academic books can one say that?"

Charles Martindale, Bristol University

Reading Poetry

The books in this series include close readings of well known and less familiar poems, many of which can be found in the Blackwell Annotated Anthologies. Each volume provides students and interested faculty with the opportunity to discover and explore the poetry of a given period, through the eyes of an expert scholar in the field.

The series is motivated by an increasing reluctance to study poetry amongst undergraduate students, born out of feelings of alienation from the genre, and even intimidation. By enlisting the pedagogical expertise of the most esteemed critics in the field, the volumes in the *Reading Poetry* series aim to make poetry accessible to a diversity of readers.

Published:

Reading Sixteenth-Century Poetry	Patrick Cheney, Penn State University
Reading Paradise Lost	David Hopkins, University of Bristol
Reading Eighteenth-Century Poetry	Patricia Meyer Spacks, University of Virginia
Reading Romantic Poetry	Fiona Stafford, Oxford University
Reading Victorian Poetry	Richard Cronin, Glasgow University
Reading Modernist Poetry	Michael Whitworth, Oxford University

Forthcoming:

Reading Shakespeare's Poetry	Dympna Callaghan, Syracuse University
Reading Seventeenth-Century Poetry	Michael Schoenfeldt, University of Michigan

Also available from Wiley-Blackwell:

The Life of John Milton: A Critical Biography
Barbara K. Lewalski

Paradise Lost
Edited by Barbara K. Lewalski

John Milton: Complete Shorter Poems
Edited by Stella P. Revard

John Milton Prose: Major Writings on Liberty, Politics, Religion, and Education
Edited by David Loewenstein

Reading *Paradise Lost*

David Hopkins

WILEY-BLACKWELL

A John Wiley & Sons, Ltd., Publication

This edition first published 2013
© 2013 John Wiley & Sons, Ltd

Wiley-Blackwell is an imprint of John Wiley & Sons, formed by the merger of Wiley's global
Scientific, Technical and Medical business with Blackwell Publishing.

Registered Office
John Wiley & Sons, Ltd, The Atrium, Southern Gate, Chichester, West Sussex, PO19 8SQ, UK

Editorial Offices
350 Main Street, Malden, MA 02148-5020, USA
9600 Garsington Road, Oxford, OX4 2DQ, UK
The Atrium, Southern Gate, Chichester, West Sussex, PO19 8SQ, UK

For details of our global editorial offices, for customer services, and for information about how
to apply for permission to reuse the copyright material in this book please see our website at
www.wiley.com/wiley-blackwell.

The right of David Hopkins to be identified as the author of this work has been asserted in
accordance with the UK Copyright, Designs and Patents Act 1988.

Library of Congress Cataloging-in-Publication Data

Hopkins, David, 1948–
  Reading Paradise lost / David Hopkins.
     p.   cm.
  Includes bibliographical references and index.
  ISBN 978-1-118-47100-5 (cloth)
1. Milton, John, 1608–1674. Paradise lost.   2. Fall of man in literature.   I. Title.
  PR3562.H66 2013
  821′.4–dc23

                                   2012034394

A catalogue record for this book is available from the British Library.

Cover image: Rubens, Adam and Eve, c.1598–1600. Rubens House, Antwerp.
Photo © The Art Archive / Alamy.

Cover design by Design Deluxe

Set in 11/13.5pt Galliard by SPi Publisher Services, Pondicherry, India
Printed and bound in Malaysia by Vivar Printing Sdn Bhd

1   2013

Contents

Preface

This book explores some of the main narrative and poetic qualities which have compelled and fascinated readers of John Milton's *Paradise Lost* for more than three centuries. Designed to be readable in a single sitting, it will, I hope, appeal both to beginners seeking some initial critical orientation, and to others wishing to refresh or extend their acquaintance with *Paradise Lost* after, perhaps, a preliminary encounter with parts of it at school or university. It may also have some interest for more experienced readers, since, though the scale and scope of the book preclude any sustained or detailed engagement with the vast body of secondary literature on *Paradise Lost*, it offers an implicit contribution to some of the most enduring and vigorously contested debates about Milton's poem.

There are already many books on *Paradise Lost*, from which readers will learn much of value. What, then, apart from its brevity, is distinctive about the present one? The best way of answering that question may be by way of a short account of the reception history of Milton's poem. This account, needless to say, is given in very broad brush-strokes, and ignores numerous local exceptions and nuances. But it is, I think, true enough in its general outlines for my present purposes.

For nearly two centuries after its appearance, *Paradise Lost* was widely admired for the grandeur and beauty of its imaginative vision, narrative sweep, and poetic language. Milton was felt to have told a story of human and cosmic significance with a mastery that rivets the reader's attention. His unique and challenging verse style, often employing blank-verse paragraphs of majestic compass, was thought to have successfully embraced the widest range of expressive effects, from awe-inspiring sublimity, through calm philosophical survey, to sensuously delicate description, and the intimate rendering of human speech. Milton was thought to have enriched the English language with resonances from his Latin, Greek, and Hebrew reading. He was believed to have created the definitive modern epic, subsuming and eclipsing the achievements in that genre of the great poets of classical antiquity and renaissance Italy. 'This man,' the poet Dryden is reported to have remarked on first reading *Paradise Lost*, 'cuts us all out – and the ancients too.'

To be sure, some of Milton's earlier readers expressed (sometimes quite severe) reservations about specific details of the design and language of *Paradise Lost*. And the poem's reputation was no doubt enhanced in a general way by the fact that it was based on subject matter – the story of the Fall of Man as narrated in the Old Testament Book of Genesis – that was central to the teachings of the Christian religion which most of its readers professed. But local quibbles did not diminish the near-universal reverence in which *Paradise Lost* was held. Nor were the poem's admirers limited to those who shared the particular doctrinal or political beliefs of its author. *Paradise Lost* gave enormous pleasure to readers of both sexes, right across the political and religious spectrum. It soon established its reputation as the single greatest non-dramatic poem in English literature.

But around the middle of the nineteenth century, things began to change. In some respects, Milton's reputation continued to grow, and his status as (in Gordon Campbell's phrase) 'the national poet' was consolidated in the publication of David Masson's vast seven-volume biography (1859–94). But doubts began to be expressed about his greatest poem. *Paradise Lost* ceased to be generally regarded as a bountiful provider of rich, diverse, and awe-inspiring poetic pleasure, and started to be seen by some as a 'problem.' The poem's Old Testament subject matter – which, it was thought, Milton had believed in as 'literal' truth – had now begun in some quarters to seem embarrassingly primitive and outmoded. How, it was asked, could Milton possibly have made a coherent and appealing narrative poem out of such a grotesquely implausible story? How could he have hoped to deal satisfactorily, in the context of a poetic narrative, with issues – such as the origins of evil, and the compatibility of human free will with divine foreknowledge and omnipotence – that had exercised, and frequently baffled, the greatest philosophers and theologians down the ages?

This mid-nineteenth-century suspicion of the poem survived into the twentieth, where it was coupled with objections to Milton's poetic language. Whereas earlier critics had admired the variety, subtlety, and sensuous richness of Milton's verse, it was now seen by some as monotonous, bludgeoning, pompously rhetorical, syntactically tortuous, and excessively Latinate. Milton was said to have violated the inherent character of the English language. Such charges were vigorously contested in some quarters, but some of the champions of Milton's language were surprisingly willing to accept the nineteenth-century objections to his poem's larger design: Milton was defended by some for the fineness of his local effects, but not for the coherence of his overall conception. In other quarters, it was conceded that admiration (or distaste) for Milton's poem was likely to go hand-in-hand with one's sympathy with (or hostility to) the religion which underpins it, and some of Milton's champions were quite willing to concede that *Paradise Lost* would be unlikely to appeal to non-Christians – unless, that is, they were willing to read the poem manifestly against its grain.

The nineteenth- and twentieth-century objections to *Paradise Lost* are nowadays commonly treated as passé. And an older-style admiration for the poem was no doubt maintained by many readers throughout the twentieth-century 'Milton controversy': ordinary readers' habits are often remarkably unaffected by the palace revolutions of the critical community. But the effects of twentieth-century anti-Miltonism linger on to a surprising degree, even in the work of those who would probably be shocked to find themselves associated with it.

Recently, discussion of *Paradise Lost*, like that of most earlier literature, has retreated within the walls of the academy, and has been primarily addressed to those studying the poem formally at school, undergraduate, or postgraduate level. Some of this discussion has continued to celebrate the poetic qualities of *Paradise Lost* in terms which would have been recognizable by the poet's early admirers. But in accordance with current academic fashion, much recent writing on Milton has been less concerned with the artistic merits or demerits of the poet's work than with the relations between that work and its 'context,' political, theological, and ideological. Indeed, in some quarters this has involved a turning away from Milton's poetry altogether, in favor of the polemical and political prose which occupied much of his career. This body of work – which, the poet said,[1] had involved 'the use ... but of [his] left hand' – had contributed significantly to Milton's high standing in Whig and republican circles in the eighteenth and early nineteenth centuries. In the quatercentenary year of Milton's birth, one journalist reflected the renewed emphasis on the poet's prose when he commented that *Paradise Lost*, with its copious references to 'a theology and mythology that today are gone,' is 'largely empty' for modern readers. 'Milton the poet,' this writer asserted, 'was a bore and a prig.' If he is to be admired today, it will not be for his verse but for his 'sensational,' and 'majestic' polemical writings, and particularly for his 'explosive defence of free speech.'[2] In the following year, another writer, reviewing a new biography of Milton, noted that the authors of this work had devoted three times as much space to one of Milton's minor pamphlets than to one of his most famous shorter poems. 'By writing so richly about the polemical prose and saying so little about the literary art,' the reviewer suggested, the biographers had given the impression that Milton will be remembered as 'a superior Salmatius rather than a figure who shaped English poetry for two centuries.'[3]

The present book is written out of three main convictions: First, that it is possible for modern readers to recapture much of the enthusiasm for the imaginative vision, narrative excitement, and poetic beauty of *Paradise Lost* that was felt by its earliest admirers. Second, that such an enthusiasm need be no more dependent than that of many of Milton's early readers on any particular sympathy with the beliefs and opinions of Milton the man, or any specialized interest in the religious and ideological conflicts of the seventeenth century. Third, that, as with any great poem, understanding *Paradise Lost* is inseparable from enjoying it. As William Empson noted, 'the act of knowing is itself an act of sympathising; unless you are enjoying the poetry, you cannot create it, as poetry, in your own mind.'[4] The present book, accordingly, concentrates on those areas of *Paradise Lost* – the depictions of Satan and God, the descriptions of Adam and Eve's life together in Eden, the portrayal of the events leading to the Fall – which might, because of some of the advance publicity they have received, present obstacles to modern readers' enjoyment, and thus understanding, of Milton's poem. The suggestion is not that Milton's poem is faultless, 'for faults and defects,' as Samuel Johnson noted, 'every work of man must have,' but, rather, that a critic's first duty is to draw attention to the strengths of his subject. 'A true critic,' wrote Joseph Addison in one of his *Spectator* papers on *Paradise Lost*, 'ought to dwell rather upon excellences than imperfections, to discover the concealed beauties of a writer, and communicate to the world such things as are worth their observation.' Such a focus, together with the need to maintain brevity, has meant that there are many important areas of *Paradise Lost* which receive no coverage in the present book. Nor does the book offer (except incidentally) basic handbook information about such matters as the circumstances of the poem's composition, or the poet's sources. The note on Further Reading gives some suggestions of books and essays which will provide such information, and which will enable readers both to develop further the issues discussed in this book, and to explore areas and aspects of the poem for which no room could be found in a study of this scale. The same note also gives offers some pointers for readers interested in pursuing some of the current concerns of Milton scholarship.

The ideas and arguments in this book have been tried out over many years in lectures and seminars at the University of Bristol. I am grateful to several generations of students, whose enthusiasm and resistance has, I hope, enabled me to refine, correct, develop, and clarify my material over the years. I am grateful to Colin Burrow, Greg Clingham, David Fairer, Charles Martindale, and Tom Mason, all of whom read the book in draft form and made useful and encouraging comments. A valuable early stimulus to my thinking about *Paradise Lost* was provided by J. R. Mason's 1987 Cambridge PhD thesis, 'To Milton through Dryden and Pope.' James Hopkins and Eric Southworth both provided usefull help on particular points. Kate Hopkins applied her discerning editorial eye to my manuscript, and Sandra Hopkins provided detailed and searching criticism at all stages throughout the book's gestation. Needless to say, none of them is responsible for the imperfections which remain. Emma Bennett at Wiley-Blackwell has been most supportive in bringing the project to its final published form.

All quotations from earlier sources have been modernized for readers' convenience. In accordance with the general nature of the book, endnotes have been kept to an absolute minimum, and references are only supplied when readers might have genuine difficulty in locating the source being referred to.

Endnotes

1 In *The Reason of Church Government* (1642).
2 Simon Jenkins, in *The Guardian*, 12 December 2008.
3 Jonathan Bate, in *The Times Literary Supplement*, 6 March, 2009. Claudius Salmatius (Claude Saumaise) (1588–1653) was the French classical scholar to whose *Defensio Regia* ('Royalist Defence') attacking the execution of Charles I (1649), Milton responded in his *Pro Populo Anglicano Defensio* ('Defence of the English People') (1651).
4 William Empson, *Seven Types of Ambiguity* (2nd edition, London, 1947), p. 248.

1

Paradise Lost: Poem or "Problem"?

Two Propositions

I begin this short exploration of *Paradise Lost* with two simple propositions, which the rest of the book will be devoted to fleshing out and, I hope, substantiating. The first proposition is that *Paradise Lost* is a narrative poem, not a work of theology, or philosophy, or political polemic, and that it works on readers' minds according to the laws and procedures of narrative poetry, not according to those which govern the other kinds of discourse. The second proposition is that discussion of *Paradise Lost* always begins to go awry when the truth of the first proposition is forgotten.

The Laws of Poetry

What do I mean by saying that *Paradise Lost* operates "according to the laws of poetry"? "Poetry," of course, is notoriously diffi-cult to define. When asked, "What is poetry?," Samuel Johnson is reported to have replied: "Why, Sir, it is much easier to say what it is not. We all *know* what light is; but it is not easy to *tell* what it is."[1] Elsewhere, however, Johnson ventured some more positive suggestions on the subject. When discussing, for example, some of the technical minutiae of versification employed by poets, he remarked:

Reading Paradise Lost, First Edition. David Hopkins.
© 2013 John Wiley & Sons, Ltd. Published 2013 by John Wiley & Sons, Ltd.

Without this petty knowledge no man can be a poet; and ... from the proper disposition of single sounds results that harmony that adds force to reason, and gives grace to sublimity; that shackles attention and governs passions.[2]

Johnson was here drawing attention to the way that the powerful emotional effects produced by poetry are the direct result of a skillful deployment of language, which is organized and patterned by poets to a far more telling and significant degree than is usual in either written or spoken language. Poets, to be sure, have regularly stressed the role of "inspiration" in the exercise of their art – the belief that they are, in some sense, in a "higher" state when composing their work than that which they command in ordinary life. Milton himself, indeed, powerfully invokes this idea when, at the beginning of Books I and VII of *Paradise Lost* he pleads for the assistance in his great task of Urania, the Greek muse of astronomy whom he identifies as the inspiring power behind the prophet-poets of the Bible.

But such inspiration goes hand in hand, Johnson's passage quoted above suggests, with a meticulous and painstaking exercise of verbal artistry. If poetic genius is, in another formulation of Johnson's, "cold" and "inert" without its capacity to "amplify" and "animate" its raw material, it is also a faculty that involves much labor of "collecting" and "combining."[3] Poets deploy the full resources of words – not only their meanings in the obvious dictionary sense, but their subtler resonances, overtones, connections, suggestions, and ambiguities. Poets are also attentive to the ways in which language has been deployed by predecessors in their art. They both absorb the language of their forebears silently into their own, and signal towards it openly by various kinds of imitation, allusion, and echo. In poetry, language is organized so as to exploit its sounds and rhythms to the full, its capacity to evoke or – so it has seemed to many – "enact" its subject matter by onomatopoeia, assonance, and other mimetic effects.[4] For this reason, poetry is best appreciated when read aloud, whether in a full vocal rendering, or to the mind's ear. It needs to be experienced sensuously and viscerally as well as intellectually. It speaks, in W. B. Yeats's famous phrase, to "the whole man – blood, imagination, intellect, running together."[5] In poetry, "form" and "content," "style" and "subject" are indivisible:

If you read the line, "The sun is warm, the sky is clear," you do not experience separately the image of the warm sun and clear sky, on the one side, and certain unintelligible rhythmical sounds on the other; nor yet do you experience them together, side by side; but you experience the one *in* the other ... Afterwards, no doubt, when you are out of the poetic experience but remember it, you may by analysis decompose this unity, and attend to a substance more or less isolated, and a form more or less isolated. But these are things in your analytic head, not in the poem, which is *poetic* experience. And if you want to have the poem again, you cannot find it by adding together these two products of decomposition; you can only find it by passing back into poetic experience. And then what you recover is no aggregate of factors, it is a unity in which you can no more separate a substance and a form than you can separate living blood and the life in the blood.[6]

Reflections of the kind summarized above have become commonplace in the discussion of poetry. But for many modern readers the term "poem" has effectively come to mean "short poem," and "poetry" today suggests a kind of writing – usually in the form of first-person reflection – that can be printed on one side, or at the very most, two or three sides, of paper. For most modern readers, the form most associated with storytelling is not poetry but the prose novel.

But Milton, of course, wrote in – and sought to extend and enrich – a tradition of narrative poetry stretching back to the great classical epics of Homer and Virgil. Narrative verse in this tradition – which enjoyed great prestige for centuries – was thought to have all the qualities associated with short poems, but many more besides. The great narrative poems were thought to have the same powers of verbal suggestiveness, animation and enactment that are found in shorter examples of poetic art. Such powers, it was felt, allowed readers of narrative verse a vivid emotional engagement with, rather than a mere intellectual comprehension of, the actions they depicted. Alexander Pope, for example, described the effect on him of Homer's *Iliad* thus:

No man of a true poetical spirit is master of himself while he reads [Homer]. What he writes is of the most animated nature imaginable; every thing moves, every thing lives, and is put in action. If a council be called or a battle fought, you are not coldly informed of what was said or done as from a third person. The reader is hurried out of himself by the force of the poet's imagination, and turns in one place to a hearer, in another to a spectator.[7]

And Pope wrote in similar terms of a much shorter and much more recent narrative poem, John Dryden's *Alexander's Feast* (1697). In that work, Dryden had imagined how Alexander the Great – the alleged son of Jupiter ("Lybian Jove") and the mightiest conqueror in the world, who has just triumphed in battle over the great Persian empire – was disconcertingly transported by the mercurial artistry of his court poet-musician Timotheus into a succession of emotional states quite beyond his control. To read Dryden's poem, Pope suggested in his *Essay on Criticism* (1711), is to feel Alexander's constantly shifting emotions with something like the irresistible immediacy experienced by the poem's "godlike hero" himself:

> Hear how Timotheus' varied lays surprise,
> And bid alternate passions fall and rise!
> While, at each change, the son of Lybian Jove
> Now burns with glory, and then melts with love;
> Now his fierce eyes with sparkling fury glow;
> Now sighs steal out, and tears begin to flow:
> Persians and Greeks like turns of nature found,
> And the world's victor stood subdued by sound!
> The power of music all our hearts allow;
> And what Timotheus was, is Dryden now.
>
> (374–83)

The great narrative poems, it was believed, did not merely reflect, reproduce, or record the world we inhabit in daily life. They could create "new worlds," inhabitable only in the imagination, drawing on the world we know but radically transforming, reconstituting, and recombining its elements. In the words of Shakespeare's Theseus in *A Midsummer Night's Dream*,

> as imagination bodies forth
> The forms of things unknown, the poet's pen
> Turns them to shapes, and gives to airy nothing
> A local habitation and a name.
>
> (V. i. 14–17)

Narrative poets could, moreover, it was believed, combine emotional states and sentiments which would normally be thought incompatible, and could make attractive and comprehensible beliefs, relationships and events which would be perplexing, even repellent, in ordinary life. The poet Shelley commented memorably on this quality in his *Defence of Poetry* (written, 1821, published 1840):

> Poetry turns all things to loveliness; it exalts the beauty of that which is most beautiful and it adds beauty to that which is most deformed; it marries exultation and horror, grief and pleasure, eternity and change; it subdues to union, under its light yoke, all irreconcilable things. It transmutes all that it touches.

Narrative poems, like dramas, it was thought, cannot be properly represented by extracts, or in parts, but work in a cumulative manner to produce their effects on the imagination. Like dramas, they contain speeches in which different characters are allowed their say, and different views are juxtaposed, without being resolved into any single perspective. In the great Preface to his edition of the works of Shakespeare (1765), Samuel Johnson noted that while Shakespeare's plays contain eminently quotable "practical axioms and domestic wisdom," "his real power is not shown in the splendour of particular passages, but by the progress of his fable and the tenor of his dialogue." In the same way, the insights of a great narrative poem, it was thought, are not located, in a detachable way, in any of its local parts – even those in which the poet apparently speaks in his own voice and offers his own commentary on the action – but in the temporally unfolding and cumulative effect of the whole, and the dramatic interplay between its descriptive passages (including the extended similes that are a such a notable feature of epic poetry) and the various "voices" which speak within it.[8] Key sentiments and ideas are returned to, and seen from different angles as the narrative progresses. Apparent digressions and interludes turn out, as one reads, to be relevant to the poem's larger concerns. Significant words – in *Paradise Lost*, for example, such apparently simple terms as "bliss," "height," "love," "naked," "reason," "sin," "sweet" – acquire further depth and resonance as the story unfolds. And at the local level, the narrative poet controls the movement, rhythm, and evocative power of his language in the way with which we have become familiar from shorter poems, thus enabling any "ideas" or "doctrines" which his work contains to affect the reader in a quite a different way from that in which similar material would affect them if encountered in a work of philosophy or theology.

Paradise Lost, this book suggests, operates as a narrative poem in the ways broadly sketched above. It achieves its objective of "justifying the ways of God to men" not by deductive reasoning or theological dogma, but by conducting us through an experiential process which conveys to us both the goodness of the divine dispensation which it imagines, and the perils of rejecting that dispensation. It allows us to live with paradoxes which in other kinds of writing would seem mere contradictions. It solicits our imaginative participation in the events which it depicts, and enables us to comprehend the sentiments of the various agents in those events with inwardness and sympathy. It brings home to us the complexities and difficulties of the choices which they face. It offers a plausible depiction of scenes, sentiments, and relationships which, in other treatments, might seem remote from human comprehension and concern. And it does all this in language that is remarkable for its variety, ranging from sublime grandeur to the most minute and sensuous delicacy.

Such a general view of Milton's poem was once commonplace. What has caused it to lose its hold? One answer, I think, might go somewhat as follows. *Paradise Lost* contains, at various points, arguments that are close to those of philosophy or theology. The poem, no less than those of Lucretius and Dante, is, indeed, full of theological and philosophical argumentation. That argumentation, moreover – about divine foreknowledge, human free will, the relations between the sexes, the origins of evil – concerns issues on which Milton himself expressed strong views in prose, and about which his readers are likely to have strong opinions of their own. It has been very easy, therefore, for commentators on *Paradise Lost* to slide from talking about Milton's ideas and arguments as they are presented in the poem into discussing them as if they were independent entities, abstractable from "the progress of the fable and the tenor of the dialogue" of *Paradise Lost*. It has also been frequently assumed that *Paradise Lost* contains much that Milton believed as literal, historical fact, but which we find quite unacceptable or ludicrous. Milton, it has been suggested, was asking us to accept and approve of a wrathful, omniscient, anthropomorphic God, and a hierarchical arrangement of the universe in which, at the centre, man and woman exist in a divinely appointed hierarchy. And he was asking us to believe in these not as fictions, symbols, myths, or metaphors, but as events with a factual, historical status.

Two French Critics and an English Poet on *Paradise Lost*

Such arguments, I would suggest, are based on serious misapprehensions about Milton's whole artistic endeavor. In support of such a proposition, let first us consider two general statements about *Paradise Lost* by critics of the past. They are both by Frenchmen of a decidedly skeptical temperament. The first is by the Enlightenment philosopher Voltaire (1694–1778), and is taken from his *Essay on Epic Poetry* (1727):

> What Milton so boldly undertook, he performed with superior strength of judgement, and with an imagination productive of beauties not dreamed of before him. The meanness, if there is any, of some parts of the subject is lost in the immensity of the poetical invention. There is something above the reach of human forces to have attempted the creation without bombast, to have described the gluttony and curiosity of a woman without flatness, to have brought probability and reason amidst the hurry of imaginary things belonging to another world, and as far remote from the limits of our notions as they are from our earth; in short, to force the reader to say, "If God, if the angels, if Satan would speak, I believe they would speak as they do in Milton."
>
> I have often admired [wondered at] how barren the subject appears, and how fruitful it grows under his hands.
>
> The *Paradise Lost* is the only poem wherein are to be found in a perfect degree that uniformity which satisfies the mind and that variety which pleases the imagination, all its episodes being necessary

lines which aim at the centre of a perfect circle. Where is the nation who would not be pleased with the interview of Adam and the angel? With the Mountain of Vision, with the bold strokes which make up the relentless, undaunted and sly character of Satan? But above all with that sublime wisdom which Milton exerts, whenever he dares to describe God and to make him speak? He seems indeed to draw the picture of the Almighty as like as human nature can reach to, through the mortal dust in which we are clouded.

The heathens always, the Jews often, and our Christian priests sometimes, represent God as a tyrant infinitely powerful. But the God of Milton is always a creator, a father, and a judge, nor is his vengeance jarring with his mercy, nor his predeterminations repugnant to the liberty of man ...

But he hath especially an undisputable claim to the unanimous admiration of mankind, when he descends from those high flights to the natural description of human things. It is observable that in all other poems love is represented as a vice; in Milton only 'tis a virtue. The pictures he draws of it are naked as the persons he speaks of, and as venerable. He removes with a chaste hand the veil which covers everywhere else the enjoyments of that passion. There is softness, tenderness and warmth without lasciviousness. The poet transports himself and us into that state of innocent happiness in which Adam and Eve continued for a short time. He soars not above human, but above corrupt nature, and as there is no instance of such love, there is none of such poetry.

The second passage is by the nineteenth-century French politician, man of letters, and one-time theologian, Edmond Scherer (1815–89), and is taken from his essay "Milton and 'Paradise Lost'" (1868):[9]

"Paradise Lost" is an epic, but it is a theological epic, and the theology of the poem is made up of the favourite dogmas of the Puritans – the Fall, Justification, the sovereign laws of God. Moreover, Milton makes no secret of the fact that he is defending a thesis: his end, he says in the first lines, is to "assert eternal providence And justify the ways of God to man."

There are, therefore, in "Paradise Lost" two things which must be kept distinct: an epic poem and a theodicy [a vindication of divine justice]. Unluckily, these two elements ... were incapable of thorough fusion. Nay, they are at complete variance, and from their juxtaposition there results an undertone of contradiction which runs through the whole work, affects its solidity and endangers its value ... Christianity is a religion which has been formally "redacted" and settled; and it is impossible, without doing it violence, to add anything to it or subtract anything from it. Moreover, Christianity is a religion serious in itself and insisting on being taken seriously, devoted to ideas the gravest, not so say the saddest, that imagination can form ...

But this is not all. Christianity is a religion of dogma: in place of the fantastic and intangible myths of which the Aryan religions were made up, it has abstruse distinctions, paradoxical mysteries, subtle teachings. In short, it amounts to a metaphysic, or, to return to the expression I used at first, a theology. And theology has never had the reputation of being favourable to poetry ...

"Paradise Lost" is not only a theological poem – two words which cry out at finding themselves united – but it is at the same time a commentary on texts of Scripture. The author has chosen for his subject the first chapters of Genesis, that is to say a story which the stoutest or the simplest faith hesitates to take quite literally, a story in which serpents are heard speaking and the ruin of the human race is seen to be bound up with a fault merely childish in appearance. In fixing on such a subject, Milton was obliged to treat the whole story as a literal and authentic history; and, worse still, to take a side on the questions which it starts. Now these questions are the very thorniest in theology; and so it comes about that Milton, who intended to instruct us, merely launches us on a sea of difficulties. What are we to understand by the Son of the Most High, who, one fine day, is begotten and raised to the rank of viceroy of creation? How are we to comprehend an angel who enters on a conflict with God, that is to say, with a being whom he knows to be omnipotent? What kind of innocence is it which does not prevent a man from eating forbidden fruit? How, again, can this fault extend its effects to ourselves? By what effort of imagination or of faith can we regard the history of Adam as part of our own history, and acknowledge solidarity with his crime in ourselves? And if Milton does not succeed in arousing this feeling in us, what becomes of his poem? What is its value, what is its interest? It becomes equally impossible to take it seriously as a profession of faith (since this faith escapes us) and even to regard it as the poetical expression of a theodicy which is out of date, because that theodicy could only become poetic on the terms of being intelligible.

(pp. 120–2)

Paradise Lost, Scherer concludes, "is an unreal poem, a grotesque poem, a tiresome poem." It does not "hold together," and the only thing that can be salvaged from the wreckage is "some episodes" which, Scherer concedes, "will be for ever famous." Milton therefore "ought not to be read except in fragments."

Voltaire and Scherer clearly differ drastically in their valuation of *Paradise Lost*. (Later in his essay, Voltaire goes on to register some reservations about parts of Milton's poem, but his dominant response remains emphatically positive.) Much of what both critics say is widely echoed, in one way or another, in criticism of Milton's poem before and after, respectively, the "great divide" in the poem's reputation which, I suggested in my Preface, occurred around the middle of the nineteenth century.

But as well as their diametrically opposed conclusions, there is, it will be noticed, a radical difference in the way that the two critics conduct their arguments. It is notable that both critics share a conspicuous lack of sympathy with the poem's raw material. But in Voltaire's view, Milton has transformed that raw material so completely that what one might have supposed before reading *Paradise Lost* would have been the most unpropitious subject matter for a narrative poem, has become, in Milton's handling, impressive, delightful, and convincing: "I have often admired how barren the subject appears, and how fruitful it grows under his hands." Scherer, in contrast, assumes from the start that a successful poem could not possibly have been made out of such unpromising material: "There are in 'Paradise Lost' two things which *must* [my emphasis] be kept apart: an epic poem and a theodicy." Voltaire is clearly articulating a first-hand response – delighted and surprised – to a work of art. Scherer assumes as his premise that such a work of art could not possibly exist.

Voltaire's combination of surprise and delight is similar to that of Milton's friend Andrew Marvell, who, in the commendatory verses printed in the second edition of *Paradise Lost* (1674), first registered his initial unease that Milton was planning an epic poem on a subject that would, it seemed, inevitably launch him on a sea of confusion and blasphemy, and then affirmed his belief that, against all the odds, Milton had succeeded in finding a style whose "majesty," "gravity," "ease" and "compass" had enabled him both to "delight" his readers, and to impress upon them the awesome "horror" of some of his subject matter:

> When I beheld the poet blind, yet bold
> In slender book his vast design unfold,
> Messiah crowned, God's reconciled decree,
> Rebelling angels, the forbidden tree,
> Heaven, hell, earth, chaos, all; the argument
> Held me a while misdoubting his intent,
> That he would ruin (for I saw him strong)
> The sacred truths to fable and old song
> (So Sampson groped the Temple's post in spite)
> The world o'erwhelming to revenge his sight.
> Yet as I read, soon growing less severe,
> I liked his project, the success did fear;
> Through that wide field how he his way should find
> O'er which lame Faith leads Understanding blind;
> Lest he perplexed the things he would explain,
> And what was easy he should render vain ....
> Pardon me, mighty poet, nor despise
> My causeless, yet not impious, surmise ....
> Thou hast not missed one thought that could be fit,
> And all that was improper dost omit: ...
> That majesty which through thy work dost reign
> Draws the devout, deterring the profane.
> And things divine thou treats of in such state
> As them preserves, and thee, inviolate.
> At once delight and horror on us seize,
> Thou sing'st with so much gravity and ease;
> And above human flight dost soar aloft
> With plume so strong, so equal, and so soft.
> The bird named from that Paradise you sing
> So never flags, but always keeps on wing.

> Where couldst thou words of such a compass find?
> Whence furnish such a vast expense of mind?
> Just heaven thee like Tiresias[10] to requite
> Rewards with prophecy thy loss of sight.
>
> (1–16, 23–4, 27–8, 31–44)

A tell-tale sign that Scherer was condemning Milton's poem on a-priori grounds is that he offered a highly questionable interpretation of the famous last words of Milton's opening invocation to his Muse, where the poet says:

> what in me is dark
> Illumine, what is low raise and support,
> That to the height of this great argument
> I may assert Eternal Providence,
> And justify the ways of God to men.
>
> (I. 22–6)

In claiming that Milton "makes no secret of the fact that he is defending a thesis," Scherer clearly assumes that by "argument" Milton means what we would mean by the word: a chain of reasoning which proceeds by systematic, logical steps. He also assumes that by "assert" Milton means something like "propose assertively, in the face of opposition, as one would in a debate or polemical pamphlet." And he clearly believes that Milton's "justify" means something like "produce a cast-iron defence against the objections of skeptics." Scherer also states unequivocally that Milton believed the Genesis story to be "a literal and authentic history."

Scherer's gloss on Milton's "justify" is, indeed, supported by one modern commentator:

> In the poet's claim that he will *justify* God's actions lies the remarkable assertion not only that he is able to do this but also that God's ways are in need of justification. Richard Baxter wrote: "Justification … implyeth Accusation" in his *Aphorismes of Justification* (London, 1649), p. 135.[11]

But the modern scholarly consensus suggests that Scherer's assumptions both about Milton's expressed intentions in his exordium, and about his beliefs concerning the truth of Scripture, are highly questionable. Scherer speaks of *Paradise Lost* as embodying "the favourite dogmas of the Puritans," including "Justification." But Milton, as is well known, emphatically rejects the Calvinistic aspect of Puritanism, putting a major emphasis throughout his poem on human free will.[12] Scherer's bias is also visible in his treatment of particular Miltonic words. This is most obvious in his implied gloss on "argument," when he says that Milton "makes no secret of the fact that he is defending a thesis." But, as one can see from Marvell's poem, by "argument," Milton simply means "the story I am about to tell." (The plot summary which Milton added in issues of his poem from 1669 is entitled "The Argument"). And "assert" seems, in the view of most of Milton's commentators, to mean not "put forward argumentatively," but "speak on the side of." Patrick Hume, Milton's first annotator (1695), noted the derivation of the word from the Latin *asserere*. Scott Elledge, the editor of the Norton Critical Edition (1993), explained that this verb originally meant "to put one's hand on the head of a slave to set him free or defend him." Hence, in *Paradise Lost*, "assert" comes to mean something like "to take the part of; to champion sympathetically." Similarly, in the view of most commentators, "justify," for Milton means not "produce a theological justification of," but something closer to "demonstrate the justice of." There is, therefore, no reason to accept Scherer's assertion that Milton thought that he was engaged in a theological argument (in the modern sense) to persuade readers of the justice of God's actions. Milton's invocation can be more plausibly seen as the expression of a hope that his poetical powers will be sufficient to enable him to tell his great story in a way that will demonstrate, in the manner proper to a narrative poem, the justice to humankind of the God depicted in the poem.

Knowing God

Moreover, when Scherer says that Milton believed the Genesis story to be "a literal and authentic history" he is seriously misrepresenting the way in which Milton and other contemporaries interpreted the "truth" of Scripture. In Book VII of *Paradise Lost*, Raphael, who has come to earth to explain God's ways to man, tells Adam that he will narrate the story of the creation of the world "so told as earthly notion can receive" (VII. 179). Raphael's words are paralleled by Milton's own explanation, in an important passage in *De Doctrina Christiana*, the theological treatise in Latin which he was composing or compiling at the same time as he was writing *Paradise Lost*, of the way in which it might be said that human beings "know God":[13]

> When we speak of knowing God, it must be understood with reference to the imperfect comprehension of man; for to know God as he really is far transcends the powers of man's thoughts, much more of his perception ... God therefore has made as full a revelation of himself as our minds can conceive, or the weakness of our nature can bear ... Our safest way is to form in our own minds such a conception of God as shall correspond with his own delineation and representation of himself in the sacred writings. For granting that both in the literal and figurative descriptions of God, he is exhibited not as he really is, but in such a manner as may be within the scope of our comprehensions, yet we ought to entertain such a conception of him, as he, in condescending to accommodate himself to our capacities, has shown that he desires we should conceive. For it is on this very account that he has lowered himself to our level, lest in our flights above the reach of human understanding, and beyond the written word of Scripture, we should be tempted to indulge in vague cogitations and subtleties .... We may be sure that sufficient care has been taken that the Holy Scriptures should contain nothing unsuitable to the character or dignity of God, and that God should say nothing of himself which could derogate from his own majesty .... Let us require no better authority than God himself for determining what is worthy or unworthy of him.
>
> (Book 1, Chapter 2, trans. Charles R. Sumner)

Milton is here setting out what was known as the "doctrine of accommodation." The passage makes clear that his sense of the "literal truth" of scripture was radically different from that of some modern Christian fundamentalists.[14] Milton clearly did not think that Scripture was "literally" true in the positivist manner that is sometimes understood today, where it is assumed, for example, that the "truth" or falsehood of Scripture could be "proved" or "disproved" by an appeal to fossil evidence or carbon dating. Like other Christians of his time, he thought that God had, as it were, composed his own fiction, had presented us with his own image, in Scripture. This made it necessary for Milton to include nothing in his poem which was flagrantly at odds with the biblical narrative. He could not, for example, make Adam eat the fruit before Eve. And, as many of his critics have noted, he had to exercise great care in choosing the words which he gives God to speak, making sure that God's utterance remained in absolute accord with Scripture and mainstream scriptural exegesis.

In some cases, Milton implements this principle with almost legalistic rigor. An interesting instance occurs in Book XI of *Paradise Lost*, where God is declaring to the angels that the fallen Adam and Eve must leave the Garden of Eden. At one point in the Book of Genesis, it seems to be envisaged that Adam might, if allowed to stay in Eden, acquire immortality by eating the fruit of the Tree of Life:

> And the Lord God said, Behold, the man is become as one of us, to know good and evil. And now lest he put forth his hand and take also of the tree of life, and eat and live for ever: Therefore the Lord God sent him forth from the Garden of Eden to till the ground, from whence he was taken.
>
> (Genesis, 3: 22–3)

But in the imagined world of *Paradise Lost* the Tree of Life has no such magic powers. It is, in the words of Milton's editor Alastair Fowler, "significative not effectual" – a symbol of the true immortality which Adam and Eve will be granted if they remain faithful, rather than a potential means of their gaining immortality against God's wishes. When Milton comes to imagine the same moment in *Paradise Lost*, he reworks the biblical passage as follows:

> Lest therefore his now bolder hand
> Reach also of the tree of life, and eat,
> And live for ever, *dream at least to live*
> *For ever*, to remove him I decree,
> And send him from the garden forth to till
> The ground whence he was taken, fitter toil.
>
> (XI. 93–8)

Milton follows Genesis closely, but his God is given a scornful additional phrase (italicized above) which makes it clear that, in this retelling, the possibility of Adam's gaining immortality by eating from the Tree of Life is a mere "dream." Milton sticks closely to the biblical wording, but supplements it significantly to square it with the imaginative world created in his own poem.

Such an example shows Milton exerting minute care not to contradict, however much he might gloss, Scripture. But such considerations did not prevent him, in other areas, from expanding, elaborating, recasting, and interpreting the Genesis narrative at great length and with great freedom in his poetic retelling. The Genesis narrative of the creation and Fall of Man takes up less than four pages in the Geneva and King James versions of the Bible. Milton's poem, in the finished, twelve-book version of 1674, is 10,565 lines and 333 pages long, and contains numerous incidents, descriptions, and sentiments that have no direct basis in the Bible. These include the narrative of the angels' revolt, which has no substantial source in canonical Scripture. And the whole characterization of Satan as a fallen angel, so central a feature of Milton's poem, derives more from the Church Fathers than from the Bible.

In the light of all this evidence, there is, I would argue, no good reason to suppose, with Scherer, that Milton's invocation, or his beliefs about the "truth" of Scripture would have necessarily produced a misconceived botch in which theological dogma and poetry would seem as incompatible as oil and water. There is no good reason, that is, to believe that there was an obvious and simple conflict between Milton's loyalty to his religion and to his art, between his perceived duties as a Christian, and his obligations as a narrative poet. Nor did Milton's early readers and commentators – two of whom, Zachary Pearce and Thomas Newton, were Anglican bishops – think that there was.

A Poem Divided Against Itself?

But the kinds of criticisms made by Scherer have continued to reverberate to this day in commentary on *Paradise Lost*. Scherer's own wariness about Milton's poem is not hard to understand.

Scherer had, in his earlier career, been a Protestant clergyman and theologian. But by the time he came to write his essay on *Paradise Lost*, he had lost his religious faith, renounced his holy orders, and adopted a free-thinking agnosticism. His essay on Milton can therefore be seen as a by-product of the "crisis of faith" that affected so many people across Europe during the mid-nineteenth century, under the impact of analytical biblical scholarship and new developments in geological and evolutionary theory. Scherer, one can suppose with confidence, had become so deeply embarrassed with the subject matter of *Paradise Lost* – which he assumed Milton believed in, simple-mindedly, as literal truth – that he could not bring himself to suppose for a moment that an imaginatively convincing poetical fiction could possibly have come out of it. His embarrassment was shared by many later commentators. A. J. A. Waldock's Paradise Lost *and its Critics* (Cambridge, 1947), for example, a work much read and commended in the mid-twentieth century, effectively repeated many of the same root-and-branch objections to Milton's enterprise. It is not surprising that admirers of Waldock's book such as F. R. Leavis and John Peter adopted a position of open hostility towards Milton. But reservations such as those voiced by Scherer and Waldock have also haunted the minds of some later commentators who have professed themselves among the poet's admirers.

Various ploys have been adopted by such commentators for evading or side-stepping the negative consequences of such reservations. Some, for example, have been prepared to admit Milton's failure to resolve the conflicts in which his enterprise involved him, but have argued that such a failure is positively stimulating for the reader. The poem, they have suggested, is enjoyable not because it resolves the tensions and conflicts which it contains, but because it provokes readers to strenuous and profitable thought about them. This was broadly the position adopted by Christopher Ricks in the Introduction to his Signet (later Penguin) edition of *Paradise Lost* (first published in 1968), and (in a much more extreme form) by John Carey in his little volume on Milton in the Literature in Perspective series (London, 1969). "*Paradise Lost*," wrote Carey, "is great because it is objectionable. It spurs us to protest" (p. 75). His account then focused almost entirely on what he saw as the poem's contradictions, absurdities, and provocative unpleasantness. More recently, others have welcomed Milton's self-divisions as evidence of a systematic "poetics of incertitude."[15]

Others again have seen a positive moral virtue in Milton's failure to carry out his expressed intentions. In the view of the most celebrated of such critics, William Empson, the God of the Judeo-Christian tradition is an evil tyrant and Milton's poem emphatically (and admirably) reveals him as such.[16] Yet another critical tactic has been to explain the apparent tensions and contradictions within the poem in terms of the distinctive processes which, in the critics' view, Milton's text provokes in its readers. In *Surprised by Sin* (New York, 1967; second edition, 1998), perhaps the most influential work of Milton criticism of the later twentieth century, Stanley Fish argued that the apparent sympathy which Milton elicits for Satan – long since thought to have been one of the ways in which *Paradise Lost* contradicts its own intentions – is a deliberate strategy whereby Milton "entraps" his readers, tempting them to sympathize with sentiments and personages in a way which, as they read on, they come to realize is sinful. The reader thus passes imaginatively through a process of fall and redemption which parallels that experienced by the poem's main characters.

Poetry and Belief

All of the approaches sketched above have undoubtedly served, in their different ways, to sharpen readers' perceptions of different elements in Milton's poem. But none of them seems to me to represent a necessary or fully satisfactory critical move. Most current readers of *Paradise Lost* are likely to be less troubled by the religious subject matter of the poem than their nineteenth- and twentieth-century predecessors – either because they have no Christian belief whatever, or because their Christianity takes a radically different form from those obtaining in former times. Without the understandable threat that the poem's raw material presented to recently lapsed Christians such as Scherer, modern readers may be better placed to read *Paradise Lost* as a poem, based on mythical material associated with a religion which is certainly part of their heritage (and in which they may, indeed, be believers), but in the details of whose specific subject matter they might not feel directly implicated. Such readers might, that is, be willing to read *Paradise Lost* as a poem whose fiction they are required to "believe in" no more – or less – than they would be willing to "believe in" the events depicted in other works of non-realistic fiction.

In his writings on *Paradise Lost*,[17] C. S. Lewis sometimes gave the opposite impression: that only those who shared Milton's (and Lewis's) Christian faith would be likely to enjoy or respect the poem. But elsewhere Lewis wrote suggestively about the ways in which works of literature can transport us outside ourselves and our own direct commitments and convictions, and invite our imaginative participation rather than any kind of absolute "belief":

> In reading imaginative work ... we should be much less concerned with altering our own opinions ... than with entering fully into the opinions, and therefore also the attitudes, feelings and total experience, of other men ....
>
> In good reading there ought to be no "problem of belief." I read Lucretius and Dante at a time when (by and large) I agreed with Lucretius. I have read them since I came (by and large) to agree with Dante. I cannot find that this has much altered my experience, or at all altered my evaluation, of either. A true lover of literature should be in one way like an honest examiner, who is prepared to give the highest marks to the telling, felicitous and well-documented exposition of views he dissents from or even abominates.[18]

Lewis's comparison of the lover of literature with "an honest examiner" perhaps gives the unfortunate impression that he thinks that literary reading should be conducted in a dispassionately detached manner. But elsewhere in the same book, Lewis makes it clear that our willingness, in the act of reading, to enter imaginatively into "other worlds" meets a basic and passionately felt human need to escape the prison of the self:

> Each of us by nature sees the whole world from one point of view with a perspective and a selectiveness peculiar to himself. And even when we build disinterested fantasies, they are saturated with, and limited by, our own psychology ... But we want to ... see with other

eyes, to imagine with other imaginations, to feel with other hearts, as well as with our own ... We therefore delight to enter into other men's beliefs ... even though we think them untrue ... It is *connaître* not *savoir*, it is *erleben*; we become these other selves. Not only nor chiefly in order to see what they are like, but in order to see what they see, to occupy, for a while, their seat in the great theatre, to use their spectacles and be made free of whatever insights, joys, terrors, wonders or merriment those spectacles reveal.[19]

Lewis's insistence that we can "delight" to enter the beliefs of others "even though we think them untrue" offers an implicit challenge both to those readers who object to *Paradise Lost* on religious grounds and to those – nowadays perhaps more numerous – who reject it on the strength of its treatment of the relations between the sexes. In the Preface to this book, I noted the current tendency of some critics to judge Milton not so much on the quality of his poetry as on the strength of his ideological beliefs. Milton perhaps receives more praise than blame these days for his republicanism. But such strong hostility is sometimes expressed to the attitudes to women that *Paradise Lost* is thought to embody and to have encouraged, that it is in danger of creating in our own time an a-priori resistance to the poem no less powerful than that which was formerly entertained for religious reasons.

In later chapters, I argue that Milton's depiction of woman in *Paradise Lost* is in fact considerably more sympathetic and appreciative than has sometimes been supposed. But I want for the moment to enlist C. S. Lewis's support for the more general principle that, before immediately castigating any poet for "views" with which we cannot "agree," we should submit ourselves to the imaginative experience of his or her work, taking it in the first instance on its own terms, and attempting to understand how the world which it depicts is imagined, and how its various elements derive from, and contribute to, the poet's larger conception. The suggestion is not that we should blandly accept all aspects of *Paradise Lost* unquestioningly, or fail to acknowledge that it contains within it strenuous debate on difficult issues. It is, rather, that we should seek, in the first instance, to grasp the "problems" with which it deals as they are treated within the poem's narrative, in all their complexity and interrelatedness, rather than in and for themselves, as quasi-separable sites of theological, philosophical, political, or sexual-political dispute. As Christopher Ricks rightly observed in the Introduction to his Signet edition, Milton "offers God's justice, not as the *donnée* of the poem, but as its subject" (p. xxiv). A. J. A. Waldock believed that, at the moment of Adam's fall, Milton presents the counterclaims of Adam's love for Eve and his duty to God unsatisfactorily, so that our sympathies lie, contrary to the poet's design, entirely with Adam. Commenting on Waldock's analysis, Ricks argued that, for us to feel Adam's agonized sense of his incompatible obligations to God and Eve, Adam and Eve's debt to God cannot be simply assumed, but has to have been "truly embodied in the poem itself" (p. xxi). Ricks, however, seemed to share Waldock's conviction that such a "true embodiment" has not occurred. But as we have seen, Voltaire – a critic no more enamored of Christianity than Ricks – thought otherwise. The hope of the present book is that if we approach *Paradise Lost* with the open-minded charitableness advocated in the passages from C. S. Lewis quoted above, we may come to feel, with Voltaire, that Milton's poem does, indeed, offer a convincing imaginative "embodiment" of its subject: that it presents us with "beauties not dreamed of before" and "transports" us into regions that, for all their apparent strangeness and unfamiliarity – even potential distastefulness – can genuinely inspire and delight us in the way to which Voltaire, and Milton's other earlier critics, paid repeated testimony.

Endnotes

1   *Boswell's Life of Johnson*, ed. George Birkbeck Hill, rev. L. F. Powell, 6 vols (Oxford, 1934–50), 3. 38.
2   Samuel Johnson, in *The Rambler*, No. 88 (1751).
3   Samuel Johnson, in the 'Life of Pope' (1781).
4   For a sophisticated defence of what is sometimes dismissed as 'the enactment fallacy', see Michael Silk, 'Language, Poetry, and Enactment', *Dialogos*, 2 (1995), 109–32.
5   W. B. Yeats, 'Discoveries', in *Essays and Introductions* (London, 1961), p. 266.
6   A. C. Bradley, 'Poetry for Poetry's Sake', in *Oxford Lectures on Poetry* (London, 1909), pp. 14–15.

7   Alexander Pope, in the Preface to *The Iliad of Homer* (1715).

8   I return to this important point in Chapter 3.

9   Edmond Scherer, 'Milton and "Paradise Lost"', in *Essays on English Literature*, trans. George Saintsbury (London, 1891), pp. 98–131. Scherer's essay was brought to the attention of English readers by Matthew Arnold, in 'A French Critic on Milton', *Mixed Essays* (1879).

10   Jupiter gave Tiresias the power of prophecy after Juno blinded him (Ovid, *Metamorphoses*, III. 336–8). Milton was blind by the time he composed *Paradise Lost*.

11   *Paradise Lost*, ed. David Scott Kastan: based on the classic edition of Merritt Y. Hughes (Indianapolis, 2005), p. 8.

12   In *Milton among the Puritans: The Case for Historical Revisionism* (Aldershot, 2010), Catherine Gimelli Martin has argued that it is misleading to describe Milton as a 'Puritan' at all.

13   On the circumstances of the composition of this treatise, see Gordon Campbell, Thomas N. Corns, John K. Hale, and Fiona J. Tweedie, *Milton and the Manuscript of* De Doctrina Christiana (Oxford, 2007).

14   Milton was here working in a long and rich theological tradition. For an instructive parallel, see, for example, Henry Chadwick's summary of St Augustine's subtle treatment of scriptural interpretation in *Augustine: A Very Short Introduction* (Oxford, 2001), pp. 37–9, 91–4.

15   See Peter C. Herman, *Destabilizing Milton*: Paradise Lost *and the Poetics of Incertitude* (London, 2005). This approach is explored further in *The New Milton Criticism*, ed. Peter C. Herman and Elizabeth Sauer (Cambridge, 2012).

16   William Empson, *Milton's God* (2nd edition, London, 1965).

17   See particularly *A Preface to* Paradise Lost (Oxford, 1942).

18   C. S. Lewis, *An Experiment in Criticism* (Cambridge, 1961), pp. 85–6.

19   *Ibid.*, pp. 137–8.

2

God, Satan, and Adam

Surveying the Whole

In his general appreciation of *Paradise Lost*, quoted in Chapter 1, Voltaire noted what he took to be the organic interconnectedness of the various elements in Milton's poem – the way that each of its parts makes its indispensable contribution to the effect of the whole:

> The *Paradise Lost* is the only poem wherein are to be found in a perfect degree that uniformity which satisfies the mind and that variety which pleases the imagination, all its episodes being necessary lines which aim at the centre of a perfect circle.

Voltaire's suggestion that every part of Milton's poem exists in a complex and delicate interrelation with every other part, and that the various characters, scenes, and sentiments evoked or presented at particular moments in the poem cannot be regarded in isolation one from another, or from Milton's larger design, is of crucial importance. In *Paradise Lost* Milton presents us with a holistically imagined world, in which every element bears a slightly different relation both to those in the world we know, and to every other element within its own world.

Voltaire, however, also noted the "variety" of *Paradise Lost*, and, as in any great work of art, the different parts of the poem do not, and should not, occupy a similar prominence and centrality in the reader's mind and memory. As Samuel Johnson put it:

Reading Paradise Lost, First Edition. David Hopkins.
© 2013 John Wiley & Sons, Ltd. Published 2013 by John Wiley & Sons, Ltd.

> In every work one part must be for the sake of others; a palace must
> have passages, a poem must have transitions. It is no more to be
> required that wit should always be blazing than that the sun should
> always stand at noon.[1]

Paradise Lost has moments of particular imaginative intensity, and
subsidiary or connecting moments or areas which supplement,
relate, and work out the implications of the more concentrated
passages. Feeling the force of any large work of art aright is very
much a matter of getting the main shape and design of the whole
appropriately established in one's mind – of giving proper emphasis
to the moments of maximum imaginative power, and, as it were,
letting the work organize itself around them. One then will not
make the mistake of allowing a subsidiary, or less satisfactory,
element, to usurp the place which is more properly and fairly
occupied by the most intense centers of imaginative interest.
Alexander Pope's advice, in such circumstances, is always worth
remembering:

> Survey the whole, nor seek slight faults to find
> Where Nature moves, and rapture warms the mind; ...
> In wit, and Nature, what affects our hearts
> Is not th' exactness of peculiar parts;
> 'Tis not a lip, or eye, we beauty call,
> But the joint force and full result of all.
> (*An Essay on Criticism*, 235–6; 243–6)

Many readers of *Paradise Lost* have, I believe, taken certain
passages of the poem in isolation, without the shape of the whole
and the force of its most vivid moments weighing on them, and have
made those passages assume a weight that they cannot properly
bear. This is particularly true in the case of Milton's treatment of
God, Satan, and Adam. The suggestion of this chapter is that, if one
feels the force of the poem's most powerfully imagined moments,
and if one attends to the full implications of the poem's unfolding
narrative, one cannot feel that Milton is ultimately on Satan's side,
whether consciously or unconsciously, or that the God of the poem
is merely presented as, in F. R. Leavis's phrase, "brute assertive

will," or that Adam and Eve before the Fall are unimpressive figures, with little power to engage our attention or interest.

Satan

It is a well-known and long-standing argument that Satan is the "unacknowledged hero" of *Paradise Lost*: that Milton was secretly drawn to admire Satan in a way that caused him to contradict the logic of his own enterprise at the most radical level. Satan, it is said, is invested with the martial valor of the classical epic heroes whom Milton admired. He is given defiantly republican sentiments which closely parallel those to be found in Milton's own political prose. He is in every way a more impressive figure than both the poem's cruel and self-defensive God, and its fragile, vulnerable human characters. Most people know William Blake's famous pronouncement (in *The Marriage of Heaven and Hell*, 1790–3) that "Milton was a true poet and of the Devil's party without knowing it." Also familiar is Shelley's pronouncement in his *Defence of Poetry*:

> Milton's Devil as a moral being is as far superior to his God as one who perseveres in some purpose which he has conceived to be excellent in spite of adversity and torture is to one who in the cold security of undoubted triumph inflicts the most horrible revenge upon his enemy, not from any mistaken notion of inducing him to repent of a perseverance in enmity, but with the alleged design of exasperating him to deserve new torments.

Shelley goes on (like William Empson in the twentieth century) to praise Milton precisely for allowing Satan to have all the best tunes. Other critics, however, have felt that Milton's sympathy with Satan was fatally damaging to the logic of his poem. In the view of F. R. Leavis, for example, it was only to be expected that Milton, whose over-reaching egotism had led him to warp the native grain of the English language in an attempt to invest it with the rhetorical monumentality of Latin, was subconsciously attracted to the arch-egotist of his own creation.[2]

Though one might point to factors in each of these distinguished writers' personal ideas and beliefs which may have influenced their view of Milton, it would, of course, be implausible to suggest that their judgments are merely and solely the result of prejudice, obtuseness or willful distortion. It is only fair to suppose that there must be features of Milton's portrayal of Satan which answer to their sense that he commanded Milton's secret sympathies – even if one is going on to argue (as I am) that their accounts of the matter are ultimately misleading.

Following the suggestions made at the beginning of this chapter, I propose that the best way of investigating the matter is to run one's mind over those parts of the poem in which Satan appears, remembering the order in which they occur in Milton's narrative, and asking: what is it that prompts Satan's rebellion against God in the first place, and what are the most poetically compelling impressions that we are offered of Satan in his fallen state? Does Milton convince us, by the particular ways in which he presents Satan in the poem, that Satan is not only grand, daringly defiant, physically impressive, and psychologically fascinating, but also a terrifyingly awesome figure who, if we are attending properly to all that Milton gives us, inspires us with fear and horror as much as anything we might want to call "sympathy."

"Sympathy" is sometimes used by literary students as a rather loose catch-all term for *any* kind of vivid engagement we feel with a fictional personage. It is certainly true that Milton allows us a fuller access to the inner workings of Satan's mind than to those of any other character in the poem. Satan, in that respect, might seem more "like us" than God, the angels, or the prelapsarian Adam and Eve. But Milton also carefully controls the degree to which we can sympathize with Satan – in the strict sense of "feel as he feels." If the poet's emphases are not heeded, one can easily indulge in a sentimentality towards Satan which the poem does not warrant.

Satan is actually, in important respects, very unlike us. To begin with, he is of superhuman size. His spear, we are told (I. 292–4) makes a ship's mast seem "but a wand." He can fly through the vast spaces of the cosmos – as he does in his journey from Hell to Earth, via the orb of the Sun, in Books II–III. He can change his shape at will. Most important of all, he is immortal. His hatred and misery are "obdurate" (fixed for ever) (I. 58). His misery is "infinite" (IV. 74). Like the other fallen angels, he is incapable of feeling "hope/That comes to all" (I. 66–7). He can experience no sexual delight or love, but only "fierce desire" (among "other torments"), and "pain of longing" (IV. 509–11). Satan, that is, lacks many of the qualities that, on virtually any definition, are among the most fundamental characteristics of humanity – the capacity for hope, love, and joy; the ability to master hatred and transcend despair; the limitations imposed by the constraints of time, space, and shape.

All this is not, of course, to deny the concomitant power of Milton's poetry to make us feel Satan as an imposing and impressive figure – resolute, commanding, glorious and majestic in appearance. Milton's whole conception of his anti-hero is, as many commentators have noted, worlds away from the horned devil of medieval wall paintings. There is no suggestion in the Bible itself that the snake-tempter of the book of Genesis is to be identified, as he is by Milton, with a fallen angel, once beloved of God, made out of His substance, and still preserving in his fallen state much of the glory and magnificence of the order of beings to which he belongs. The rhythms of Milton's verse clearly invite us to feel the awesomeness of Satan's bold resolve as he sets off through Chaos in Book II, and he is compared to the most valiant voyager-heroes of Greek myth, Jason and Ulysses:

> Satan stayed not to reply,
> But glad that now his sea should find a shore,
> With fresh alacrity and force renewed
> Springs upward like a pyramid of fire
> Into the wild expanse, and through the shock
> Of fighting elements, on all sides round
> Environed wins his way; harder beset
> And more endangered than when Argo passed
> Through Bosphorus betwixt the justling rocks,
> Or when Ulysses on the larbord shunned
> Charybdis, and by th' other whirlpool steered.
> So he with difficulty and labour hard
> Moved on, with difficulty and labour he.
> (II. 1010–22)

The significant positioning of "Springs upward" at the beginning of the fourth line of this passage tellingly suggests the vigor of Satan's movement, and the labored repetitions of the final lines mimic, in an equally memorable way, the resolve and endurance he displays in his arduous endeavor.

Milton's depiction of Satan allows us to hold paradoxical and contrary impressions of his personage in tension. Though ultimately to be deplored, Satan's vitality and life, as displayed in passages such as that just quoted, are vividly experienced as one reads, not straightforwardly dismissed or discounted. Where Leavis saw a fatal lack of self-knowledge in Milton's portrayal, it is surely possible to see, rather, a profound diagnostic recognition on Milton's part of the potentially satanic assertiveness and resolve in himself. The poet Coleridge (whose lecture notes on *Paradise Lost* contain some of the most insightful and memorable things ever said about the poem) noted Milton's "intense egotism" in creating all the characters in his poem out of himself – but meant the term as a compliment:

> In the Paradise Lost ... it is Milton himself whom you see; his Satan, his Adam, his Raphael, almost his Eve – are all John Milton; and it is a sense of this intense egotism that gives me the greatest pleasure in reading Milton's works. The egotism of such a man is a revelation of spirit.[3]

It is thus that we might understand Milton's attribution to Satan, via a series of allusions and verbal echoes, not only of the valor of a classical epic hero, but also of the sentiments of a seventeenth-century republican.[4] Milton associates Satan with the classical epic poetry and revolutionary political sentiments which were both close to his heart. But he also, and simultaneously, imbues his portrayal of Satan with the reservations which he felt about the ultimate worth of pagan heroism, expressed both in the rejection of classical epic at the beginning of Book IX of *Paradise Lost* and in the comprehensive denunciations of pagan antiquity in Book IV of *Paradise Regained*. And he invests Satan's speeches with his sense of how the fine sentiments of republican polemic could so easily slide into an advocacy of the very kind of monarchical tyranny that it was designed to challenge.

Why does Milton's Satan rebel against his God in the first place? Satan's crimes, as God explains in Book III (204–6), are that he "affected Godhead" and "broke his fealty" – that is, the bond of loyalty which he owes to God. When God promotes his Son to the highest glory in heaven, Satan, who "feels vigor divine within him" (VI. 157–8), and who is proudly conscious of his affinity with God, refuses (in an unexplained act of tragic blindness) to pay the required honor to his new Lord. He is suddenly consumed with a feeling, like that of Achilles reacting to Agamemnon's seizure of his captive slave-girl in Homer's *Iliad*,[5] that the Son has "engrossed" what is properly due to him (V. 775) – that is, that the Son has taken unto himself, monopolistically, the honor and glory which Satan considers to be his own due. He thereby puts himself in irreconcilable conflict with God's destined order – the ultimate reality of existence, as defined in the poem.

The universe presented in *Paradise Lost* consists of an enormous chain, or, rather, an organically interconnected process, in which all parts relate to one another in a series of hierarchically patterned relationships. The difference between the hierarchies of Milton's poem and those to which we are accustomed is that Milton's hierarchies exist without any felt oppression, or resentment of the "higher" party by the "lower." Indeed, in the world imagined in *Paradise Lost* the "lower" party is seen as realizing its own potential life more fully and perfectly *because of* its subordination. That this was true of Satan's life in Heaven before his fall is made quite clear by Satan himself in his great soliloquy at the beginning of Book IV:

> He deserved no such return
> From me, whom he created what I was
> In that bright eminence, and with his good
> Upbraided none; nor was his service hard.
> What could be less than to afford him praise,
> The easiest recompense, and pay him thanks,
> How due! Yet all his good proved ill in me,
> And wrought but malice; lifted up so high
> I 'sdained subjection, and thought one step higher
> Would set me highest, and in a moment quit
> The debt immense of endless gratitude,

So burdensome still paying, still to owe;
Forgetful what from him I still received,
And understood not that a grateful mind
By owing owes not, but still pays, at once
Indebted and discharged; what burden then?
                                        (42–57)

The elaborate paradoxes of the last lines in this passage capture Satan's realization that God's dispensation is, indeed, one in which service is perfect freedom. They also show Satan's realization that to go against the grain of God's order is to commit oneself to a permanent Hell of alienation. As an abstract notion, transported outside the poem and applied to conditions other than those which obtain in its distinctive imagined world, the hierarchical order of Milton's God might sound merely like a theological rationale for the maintenance of an exploitative status quo. But poetry is capable of rendering acceptable and attractive relationships and orders of existence which in another context might seem incredible or suspect. Milton, as a committed republican and outspoken apologist for the execution of King Charles I, was emphatically no lover per se of hierarchies claiming divine sanction. It is only in a very particular context that he offers such a hierarchy as something to be admired. Milton's main way of inviting us to accept the "rightness" of God's regime, moreover, is not to expound its principles in the abstract, but to fill our imaginations with a whole series of images and incidents in which we are shown two beings (the prelapsarian Adam and Eve) living in accord with God's ordinance, and in which we also witness the behavior and are made privy to the thoughts of a potentially magnificent personage (Satan) who has resolved to breach, irrevocably, with the divine.

It is Abdiel, the courageous angel who refuses to join Satan's rebellion who, in Book VI, passes the poem's most telling verdict on Satan's conduct:

Unjustly thou deprav'st it with the name
Of servitude to serve whom God ordains,
Or nature; God and nature bid the same,
When he who rules is worthiest, and excels
Them whom he governs. This is servitude,

> To serve the unwise, or him who hath rebelled
> Against his worthier, as thine now serve thee,
> Thy self not free, but to thy self enthralled.
>
> (VI. 174–81)

Coming where it does in the narrative, that is, I think, a thrilling and inspiring moment, both because of our sense of the noble courage of Abdiel, standing up alone against such formidable and scornful adversaries, and because we recognize that what Abdiel says is true, *having seen it for ourselves*. The narrative of *Paradise Lost* is constructed with a central "flashback": those parts of the poem where Raphael tells Adam and Eve about God's creation of the world, and narrates the story of the angels' rebellion. On the formal level, of course, this imitates the structure of Homer's *Odyssey* and Virgil's *Aeneid*, and thus forms part of Milton's stated intention both to subsume and surpass the pagan epics of classical antiquity. But the narrative structure of *Paradise Lost* is also profoundly functional, in that it allows us to see the state of the fallen angels in Hell *before* we are taken to the Garden of Eden (which Satan has pledged to corrupt), and *before* we are given an account of the earlier stages of the angels' rebellion, and of Abdiel's courageous stand. We are thus well placed by Book VI to judge the aptness of Abdiel's words.

It has sometimes been suggested that Satan's opening soliloquy in Book IV, part of which is quoted above, signals a change in Milton's treatment of Satan, a deliberate attempt on the poet's part to denigrate and reduce the stature of the glorious figure he had created in the first two books, and who was thus endangering the coherence of his poem. But the change can be attributed not to nervous second thoughts on Milton's part, but, rather, to the transformation of Satan's position caused by his new situation. He is now on his own, without the pressure to preserve his dignity in the eyes of his fellow rebels. The inner torture which coexists with the bold valour can now be allowed full play in Satan's agonized self-revelations:

> Which way I fly is Hell, my self am Hell,
> And in the lowest deep a lower deep
> Still threatening to devour me opens wide,
> To which the Hell I suffer seems a heaven.
>
> (IV. 75–8)

And again:

> Aye me, they little know
> How dearly I abide that boast so vain,
> Under what torments inwardly I groan;
> While they adore me on the throne of Hell,
> With diadem and sceptre high advanced
> The lower still I fall, only supreme
> In misery.
>
> (IV. 85–92)

Satan's words here have something of the effect with which we are familiar from the soliloquies of tragic protagonists,[6] in that they keep open the possibility that Satan just might, even now, repent, while we know, simultaneously and paradoxically, that he will not. The very intimacy with which we are allowed to enter Satan's consciousness at this point prevents us, I think, from considering him as a mere automaton, a puppet whose repentance God has arbitrarily decreed *cannot* occur. His mode of speech creates the powerful impression that repentance is still a possibility, but one that he willfully rejects.

The inner hell that the soliloquy reveals is not, however, entirely new, and has, in fact, been constantly present in the earlier books, which have vividly impressed upon us, in a series of striking and memorable images, the cost of Satan's decision to estrange himself from "God and nature." Here he is, surveying his new realm of Hell in Book I:

> his doom
> Reserved him to more wrath: for now the thought
> Both of lost happiness and lasting pain
> Torments him; round he throws his baleful eyes
> That witnessed huge affliction and dismay
> Mixed with obdúrate pride and steadfast hate.
>
> (I. 53–8)

Satan's inner despair is tellingly captured in his outward demeanor ("round he *throws* his baleful eyes"). His powerful resolve and defiance are an outward manifestation of the way in which he has willed himself to forget or suppress the despair and agony that he feels within, the sense that, because of his breach with, and denial of, the divine and natural order, he can never know hope, ease, tranquility, joy or relations – other than those of domination or perverted lust – with anything or anybody beyond himself. In another of his comments on *Paradise Lost*, Coleridge described how Satan's will is:

> the more hopeless as the more obdurate by its subjugation of sensual impulses, by its superiority to toil and pain and pleasure; in short, by the fearful resolve to find in itself alone the one absolute motive of action, under which all other motives from within and without must be either subordinated or crushed.[7]

Those remarks go a long way towards explaining why the figure of Satan in the poem might strike readers as simultaneously magnificent and terrifying. As Satan surveys his army, his very feelings of triumph are inextricable from his self-absorption:

> his heart
> Distends with pride, and hardening in his strength
> Glories.
>
> (I. 571–3)

Satan's troops are catalogued. Then their leader is described:

> he above the rest
> In shape and gesture proudly eminent
> Stood like a tower; his form had yet not lost
> All her original brightness, nor appeared
> Less than archangel ruined, and th' excess
> Of glory obscured.
>
> (I. 589–94)

Wordsworth told William Hazlitt that he could read this description until "he felt a certain faintness come over his mind from a sense of beauty and grandeur."[8] Both sets of lines quoted above offer classic demonstrations of the way that Milton has combined in the figure of Satan a heroic magnificence with a chilling destructiveness. There is a powerful metaphorical charge in the word "hardening" in the first passage, particularly in combination with the way in which

"Glories" (thrown for emphasis, as key words so often are in Miltonic blank verse, to the beginning of the line) captures Satan's triumphantly defiant stance. And "hardening" chimes with the rest of the imagery associated with Satan and the fallen angels, which gathers momentum throughout the opening books – imagery of fire, steel, chains, armor. Theirs is a world of hard textures, harsh sounds, and pungent heat – the heat of Hell's fires, but also of the torments which burn them from within. They are insulated by their obdurate will and by their hard armor plating from any possibility of openness, tenderness, mutuality.

It is significant – and entirely characteristic of the way in which *Paradise Lost* constantly works by means of significant narrative and verbal juxtapositions and contrasts – that Satan is made most fully aware of his own inner hell when he is brought face to face with the beings who represent most fully the joyful reciprocity from which he has permanently alienated himself. Seeing Adam and Eve together for the first time in Eden, Satan turns aside in agony:

> Sight hateful, sight tormenting! Thus these two
> Imparadised in one another's arms
> The happier Eden, shall enjoy their fill
> Of bliss on bliss, while I to Hell am thrust,
> Where neither joy nor love, but fierce desire,
> Among our other torments not the least,
> Still unfulfilled with pain of longing pines.
> (IV. 505–11)

Similar thoughts beset him later in the poem:

> the more I see
> Beauties about me, so much more I feel
> Torment within me, as from the hateful siege
> Of contraries; all good to me becomes
> Bane, and in Heav'n much worse would be my state.
> (IX. 119–23)

And when he comes upon Eve alone in Book IX, he is so nonplussed by her spellbindingly graceful presence that he is momentarily halted in his dire mission, but then reinforced (in a way powerfully underlined by the change in movement in Milton's verse after the first four lines) in his will to destroy that in which he can never share:

> That space the Evil One abstracted stood
> From his own evil, and for the time remained
> Stupidly good, of enmity disarmed,
> Of guile, of hate, of envy, of revenge;
> But the hot hell that always in him burns,
> Though in mid heaven, still ended his delight,
> And tortures him now more, the more he sees
> Of pleasure not for him ordained.
>
> (IX. 463–70)

God

Objections to Milton's portrayal of God in *Paradise Lost* tend to concentrate on those moments in the poem in which God appears in person, and particularly on those passages with a heavily theological content, such as the long speech near the beginning of Book III, where God describes how Adam and Eve will succumb to Satan's temptation, and explains that the fact that He foreknows that this will happen is not the same as His having caused it to happen. These are clearly the parts of the poem which presented Milton with his most formidable challenge, since, in bringing God directly into the action and giving him words to speak, the poet inevitably imbued him with aspects of human psychology which might seem incompatible with an omniscient and omnipotent divine being. In his speeches, indeed, God has seemed to many to be all too human, or all too like the God of the Old Testament: ill-tempered, defensive, vindictive. Alexander Pope memorably highlighted the problem of having God himself adopt the role of a theologian within a poem designed to display His justice:

> Milton's strong pinion now not Heav'n can bound,
> Now serpent-like, in prose he sweeps the ground,
> In quibbles, angel and archangel join,
> And God the Father turns a school divine.
>
> (*The First Epistle of the Second Book of Horace, Imitated*, 99–102)

In his *Spectator* papers on *Paradise Lost* (1712), Joseph Addison noted that in the passages in the poem where God is introduced as a speaker, Milton's poetic imagination seems constrained by the need to stick closely to Scripture and to the writings of "the most orthodox divines."[9] And C. S. Lewis even wished that Milton had left God as a mysterious and vague figure, rather than as the forthright orator who appears in his poem.

Can Milton be defended against such criticisms? One must immediately concede that bringing God "on stage" was bound to involve a certain awkwardness for the duration of those passages in which He appears in person and speaks. The matters treated by God in the speech, to be sure, induce rapid intellectual vertigo when pondered in the abstract. The awkward questions proliferate. How *can* an omnipotent and omniscient God who knows what is going to happen not be said to have caused what happens? If God knows that Adam and Eve will fall, why did he not make them perfect (and thus unsusceptible to falling) from the start? These were questions that much preoccupied Milton's younger contemporary, John Dryden, and which Dryden turned to searchingly skeptical and comic effect in some of his own work.[10] But the direct portrayals of God only represent one part – and, poetically speaking, the least interesting and convincing part – of what "God" represents in the poem. It was clearly necessary for Milton's overall design that the God of *Paradise Lost* should be presented as a personal God, with whom other figures – the Son, the angels, Adam and Eve – can have direct relations and conversation. For this reason, it was impossible for Milton to represent God merely as the mysterious, numinous presence desired by Lewis. And Milton's commitment to God's "accommodation" of himself to human understanding in Scripture (discussed in Chapter 1) obliged him to follow the scriptural portrayal of the Deity in all His wrathful self-righteousness.

But the scenes in which God appears in person are not the only means whereby Milton conveys God's nature to his readers. If one allows due weight to the most imaginatively vivid moments in *Paradise Lost*, it would seem that God's goodness is primarily established in the poem not by what He *says* about it, but by the way that goodness is dramatized in "the progress of the fable and the tenor of the dialogue." Those who judge Milton's God harshly often seem to have concentrated exclusively on some of the passages in which God speaks, and to have allowed vast tracts of the poem – the parts in which God's good works are brought home to our imaginations most vividly – to have dropped out of their minds and memories entirely.

Free Will

God's notorious speech in Book III is perhaps best thought of as the skeletal exposition of truths which are more extensively and adequately embodied elsewhere in the poem, and which, indeed, depends on that embodiment for it to be fully understood. Large areas of Milton's poem are devoted not so much to expounding or debating the basis of God's justice, but to showing us the practical, experiential consequences of God's decisions, and to making us feel the beauty of God's creation, the beneficence of His gift of free will, and the righteousness of His harsh abasement of his enemies. God's justice in the poem, that is, is not something which is merely asserted or postulated, or which merely depends on a prior investment of faith, but something which is embodied in many hundreds of lines of verse, through action, description, and conversation.

Earlier, when discussing Satan's soliloquy at the beginning of Book IV, I suggested that we do not feel that, when Satan declares his unwillingness to repent, he is behaving as a mere automaton, deterministically constrained to evil by a higher power. We are made to believe that Satan genuinely has the option of repenting, but willfully refuses, because he "disdains" the "submission" which repentance would involve. I do not think that this feeling is invalidated by God's pronouncement in Book III:

> The first sort [i.e. the fallen angels] by their own suggestion fell,
> Self-tempted, self-depraved: man falls deceived
> By the other first: man therefore shall find grace,
> The other none.
>
> (III. 129–32)

When we come to Book IV, we do not, I suggest, feel that Satan simply has no chance of repenting since God has already told us that he "shall" find no grace. The poem convinces us, at this moment, that Satan's rebellious resolve is freely chosen, and that his will is "not overruled by Fate / Inextricable, or strict necessity" (V. 527–8).

Likewise, in the scene in Book VIII where Adam, after his creation, asks God for a companion with whom he can share his life in Eden, I do not think, if we are responding attentively to the passage, that the dialogue strikes us as merely rigged: God simply putting words into Adam's mouth so that He can then praise Adam for saying what He had made him say in the first place. Adam's boldly independent response to God's initial, teasing puzzlement that he should need companionship testifies impressively to the self-knowledge and freedom of mind and spirit which we have been told (IV. 294–5; V. 524–34; VII. 508–10) mark out humankind as the crown of God's creation. Adam's words have that stately, measured command and precision of address that are characteristic of his speech throughout the poem. At this point we surely feel Adam's free will being exercised as the blessed gift of God, and would not wish things otherwise:

> Among unequals what society
> Can sort, what harmony or true delight?
> Which must be mutual, in proportion due
> Giv'n and received; but in disparity
> The one intense, the other still remiss
> Cannot well suit with either, but soon prove
> Tedious alike: of fellowship I speak
> Such as I seek, fit to participate
> All rational delight, wherein the brute
> Cannot be human consort.
>   (VIII. 383–92)

As with other passages already discussed, the positioning of the speech is crucial – that is, *after* our first-hand experience of the phenomena to which it alludes. Just before Adam's dialogue with God, we have seen and heard Adam's delighted first apprehensions of the workings of his newly created person. We have witnessed the pleasure which

Adam took in the motions of his own supple, naked body, we have seen how his intuitively rational spirit had immediately prompted him to look up to the heavens, on the assumption that some beneficent power greater than himself must have been responsible for the blissful state in which he has been placed. Throughout Books IV–VIII we have witnessed, at great length and in great detail, in the descriptions of Adam and Eve's life together in Eden, the beauties and pleasures of the "rational delight" (for Milton a key collocation) and "enormous bliss" of the human "society" to which Adam refers in his words to God.

Our experience of Eden also presses upon us when Raphael, asked by Adam to explain the mysteries of the planetary motions, warns Adam that such speculation should not go too far, since

> the rest
> From man or angel the great Architect
> Did wisely to conceal, and not divulge
> His secrets to be scanned by them who ought
> Rather admire;
>
> (VIII. 71–5)

Later, Raphael exhorts Adam:

> Solicit not thy thoughts with matters hid,
> Leave them to God above, him serve and fear;
> Of other creatures, as him pleases best,
> Wherever placed, let him dispose: joy thou
> In what he gives thee, this Paradise
> And thy fair Eve; Heav'n is for thee too high
> To know what passes there; be lowly wise:
> Think only what concerns thee and thy being.
> Dream not of other worlds, what creatures there
> Live, in what state, condition, or degree,
> Contented that thus far hath been revealed
> Not of earth only but of highest Heaven
>
> (167–78)

Samuel Johnson praised the wisdom of these speeches of Raphael: "Raphael's reproof of Adam's curiosity after the planetary motions," he wrote, "may be confidently opposed to any rule of life which any poet has delivered."[11] Raphael's sentiments are sometimes said by commentators to draw on two passages in Ecclesiastes concerning the inscrutability and unknowableness of God. But a still closer source is to be found in the Latin poet Horace, who in one of the most celebrated of his *Odes* (III. 29. 29–30) had described how "God in his providence hides future events in murky darkness." When he came to translate Horace's Ode a decade after Milton's death, Dryden interestingly echoed the phrasing of the Miltonic Raphael:

> But God has, wisely, hid from humane sight
> The dark decrees of future fate;
> And sown their seeds in depth of night;
> He laughs at all the giddy turns of state;
> When mortals search too soon, and fear too late.
>> ('Horace. Ode 29. Book 3, Paraphrased
>> in Pindaric Verse', 45–9)

Horace's suggestion is that it is futile and foolish for man to seek to know more than God, or the gods, have revealed to them. Milton's Raphael transforms and extends Horace's moral, arguing that it is sinful, rather than merely foolish, for human beings to press beyond the conditions which constitute their own humanity. Rather than reaching for a perspective which can only be God's, Adam should, rather, focus on the palpable delights that have been granted to humankind. Such advice might sound, at first, like a mere prohibition or restriction. But it is significant that Adam receives Raphael's words with joyful acquiescence:

> How fully hast thou satisfied me, pure
> Intelligence of heaven, angel serene,
> And freed from intricacies, taught to live
> The easiest way, nor with perplexing thoughts
> To interrupt the sweet of life, from which
> God hath bid dwell far off all anxious cares,
> And not molest us, unless we ourselves
> Seek them with wandering thoughts and notions vain.
>> (VIII. 180–7)

We are prepared to acknowledge that Adam's response is more than mere submissive passivity, partly because we remember the "wandering mazes" of "vain wisdom" and "false philosophy" in which the fallen angels became "lost" in their debates after Satan's departure in Book II (555–69), but also because, as in the conversation between Adam and God discussed earlier, we have already witnessed for ourselves, at great length, Adam and Eve's life together in Eden. So, when Raphael counsels Adam to "joy" in what God has given him – "this Paradise/And thy fair Eve" – we know precisely what such an injunction entails. For it is in his descriptions of Eden and creation in the central books of the poem that Milton has conveyed most fully and richly his sense of the beneficence of God's dispensation and, by implication, the wickedness of any power that sets itself against such a dispensation. It is, therefore, to these parts of the poem – its radiant imaginative core – that we must now turn.

Endnotes

1 'Life of Milton' (1779).
2 See his two essays on Milton in *The Common Pursuit* (London, 1952); Leavis's strictures on Milton's language are voiced in *Revaluation* (London, 1936).
3 *Coleridge on the Seventeenth Century*, ed. R. F. Brinkley (Durham NC, 1955), p. 587.
4 For the classical echoes, see Charles Martindale, *John Milton and the Transformation of Classical Epic* (London, 1986); for Satan's republican rhetoric, see Blair Worden, 'Milton's Republicanism and the Tyranny of Heaven,' in *Machiavelli and Republicanism*, ed. Gisela Bock, Quentin Skinner, and Murizio Viroli (Cambridge, 1990), pp. 225–45.
5 For the use of Homer here, see Colin Burrow's chapter on Milton in *Epic Romance: Homer to Milton* (Oxford, 1993) and my chapter on 'Milton and the Classics', in Paul Hammond and Blair Worden (eds), *John Milton: Life, Writing, Reputation* (Oxford, 2010).
6 Milton's nephew Edward Phillips reported that the soliloquy, indeed, started life as a dramatic speech, when Milton was thinking of casting the material of *Paradise Lost* as a play. Commentators have compared

the first passage quoted above with Mephistopheles' words in Marlowe's *Dr Faustus* (A text, I. iii. 78): 'Why, this is hell, nor am I out of it.'

7   Brinkley, *Coleridge on the Seventeenth Century*, pp. 591–2.

8   *The Critical Opinions of William Wordsworth*, ed. Markham L. Peacock, Jnr (Baltimore, 1950), p. 311.

9   See *The Spectator*, No. 315 (on Book III).

10   See his 'operatic' version of *Paradise Lost, The State of Innocence* (1677), and his use of Milton in *The Cock and Fox*, his translation of Chaucer's *Nun's Priest's Tale*, as described by Taylor Corse in *Milton Quarterly*, 27 (1993), 109–18, and Tom Mason in *Translation and Literature*, 16 (2007), 1–28.

11   Samuel Johnson, 'Life of Milton.'

3

Eden

Changing Views of Milton's Eden

The descriptions of Eden, and of Adam and Eve's life together before the Fall are the parts of *Paradise Lost* where the sharpest disagreement is observable between the comments of critics before and after the "great divide" in Milton criticism referred to in the Preface and Chapter 1 of this book. For most of Milton's earlier critics, the scenes in Eden were the imaginative heart of Milton's enterprise, on which everything else in the poem depended. In their *Explanatory Notes and Remarks on Milton's Paradise Lost* (1734), the Jonathan Richardsons (father and son) judged that in Milton's poem

> a more beautiful idea is given of Nature than any poet has pretended to; Nature as just come out of the hand of God, in its virgin loveliness, glory, and purity; and the human race is shown, not as Homer's, more gigantic, more robust, more valiant, but without comparison more truly amiable, more so than by the pictures and statues of the greatest masters.
>
> (pp. clix–clx)

And in his *Spectator* papers on *Paradise Lost*, Joseph Addison wrote that

> Milton's exuberance of imagination has poured forth ... a redundancy [superabundance] of ornaments on this seat of happiness and innocence ... There is scarce a speech of Adam and Eve in the whole poem, wherein the sentiments and allusions are not taken

Reading Paradise Lost, First Edition. David Hopkins.

from their delightful habitation. The reader, during their whole course of action, always finds himself in the walks of Paradise.

Even Samuel Johnson, who ultimately judged that the life which Adam and Eve enjoy together is so remote from any which we could know that "a want of human interest" is felt, in fact wrote appreciatively about Milton's portrayal:

> To Adam and Eve are given, during their innocence, such sentiments as innocence can generate and utter. Their love is pure benevolence and mutual veneration; their repasts are without luxury, and their diligence without toil. Their addresses to their maker have little more than the voice of admiration and gratitude. Fruition left them nothing to ask, and innocence left them little to fear.[1]

But in the twentieth century E. M. W. Tillyard famously quipped that "Milton, had he been stranded in his own Paradise, would very soon have eaten the apple ... and immediately justified the act in a polemical pamphlet."[2] And John Carey, in the book mentioned in Chapter 1, offered a comprehensively negative account of Milton's depictions of Eden:

> Milton has not been able to make life in Paradise seem happy or beautiful. It has formality without grace. "Our Grand Parents" deport themselves gravely among its bric-à-brac – "enamell'd colours", "Sapphire Fount", "crystal mirror". The cash-values which dictate the gold ornamentation of Heaven denaturalise Eden too, where flowers harden to a "rich inlay ... more colour"d than with stone/Of costliest Emblem". Even the apple-peel is gold. There is not a real tree or flower in the place ....
> The stately titles Adam and Eve pass back and forth ... prohibit conversational interplay ... Perhaps Milton could not make Adam ride a horse, but he does not even run or jump[3] or climb a tree ... Though supposedly young enough to start a family, he and Eve are crushingly unvivacious. They laugh only once – at an elephant's trunk.
>
> (pp. 103–4)

Milton's Evocations of Paradise

The Eden scenes are, indeed, the parts of *Paradise Lost* by which the poem must stand or fall. Positive accounts of *Paradise Lost* have maintained that they, together with the account of creation in

Book VII, are the passages where Milton has lavished all the resources of his poetic art on conveying to his readers' imaginations a direct and vivid sense of the goodness of his God's dispensation. Coleridge felt that it was fortuitous that Milton had concentrated his efforts on embodying God's bounty in Eden – the home which He has created for humankind – rather than on depicting God's own abode in Heaven: "Minute Landscapes of Paradise," Coleridge recorded in his lecture notes, " – no attempt to describe Heaven: judgement."[4] If the scenes in Paradise fail to touch our hearts, minds, and senses, then we will undoubtedly have a greatly diminished sense of the danger of the threat presented by Satan, and a commensurate reluctance to believe that anything of real importance is at stake for Adam and Eve at the moment of the Fall.

That is, however, precisely the position that some of Milton's critics have adopted. As we have seen, they have judged that Eden is a bore, that Milton secretly found it a bore – or was incapable of making it seem anything other than a bore – and that the most interesting and involving parts of the poem are therefore those which depict Adam and Eve in the fallen state we all know. But if they are right, then surely the poem's whole purpose and imaginative coherence falls apart, and, as Edmond Scherer thought, little of value can be salvaged from the wreckage apart from isolated poetic beauties?

The general challenge which faced Milton in writing the scenes in Eden is clear enough. The poet had to describe a world, and a human couple, quite different from any that his readers had known, or ever could know, but which would nevertheless speak powerfully to those readers' postlapsarian hopes, dreams, yearnings, and anxieties; which would touch their imaginations, and involve their sympathies in the events and personages being portrayed. The imagined world of Milton's Eden necessarily contains elements from the world with which we are familiar. But these are juxtaposed, fused and combined in a way that, while leaving them in some senses recognizable, transforms them into something significantly different from anything directly available from our experience.

In Milton's depiction, the whole of creation before the Fall is permeated by a vibrant, ever-moving life-force, a great spirit, at once vividly sensual and spiritually pure, that rolls through all things. The landscapes of Eden combine the wild profusion of nature with the richly ordered design of a work of art. "Inanimate" nature is imbued by Milton's poetry with an animate life, so that all parts of creation seem to have an independent vitality, and to take spontaneous pleasure in their own existence. Eden is luxurious "wilderness" of "flowering odours" and "sweets," for

> Nature here
> Wantoned as in her prime, and played at will
> Her virgin fancies, pouring forth more sweet,
> Wild above rule or art; enormous bliss.
> (V. 293–7)

In the words of A. J. Smith, Milton "shows us a creation delighting in its own right activity, as if delight itself is the active spirit in which nature works, and the natural accompaniment of its proper functioning."[5]

The first impression that Satan gets of Eden, as he flies down from the Orb of the Sun on his fatal expedition, is of an enormous mound whose sides are covered with impressively tall trees that rise upwards and upwards in ever-ascending ranks:

> Yet higher than their tops
> The verdurous wall of paradise up sprung:
> Which to our general sire gave prospect large
> Into his nether empire neighbouring round.
> And higher than that wall a circling row
> Of goodliest trees loaden with fairest fruit,
> Blossoms and fruit at once of golden hue
> Appeared, with gay enamelled colours mixed;
> On which the sun more glad impressed his beams
> Than in fair evening cloud, or humid bow,
> When God hath showered the earth; so lovely seemed
> That landscape.
> (IV. 142–53)

"I think," comments J. M. Newton,

our spines straighten as we read. ... we begin to recognise why the vigorous upthrusting of the trees is an indispensable part of Paradise's wealth of life, in Milton's rendering, when we recognise that without it all the rich fruits and scents would be too simply luxurious. The poet wouldn't be able to suggest so convincingly as he does that these are the creation of God, pleasing to Him, and extraordinarily pure as well as rich. As it is, the vigour is *in* the fruit.

To justify that last remark, Newton quotes three lines from a little further on in Milton's description –

> And all amid them [i.e. the trees] stood the Tree of Life,
> High eminent, blooming ambrosial fruit
> Of vegetable gold.
>
> (IV. 218–20)

– and comments:

> The position of the words helps to give the fact that the tree's great height is something that it has vigorously grown up to, and that the bold substitution of "blooming" for "bearing" turns the fruit into what fruit partly is, the final result of the wonderful shooting forth of the tree's life.[6]

The fruit is at one and the same time blossom (for here all seasons are as one, and the life-giving processes of nature are all happening simultaneously), and combines, miraculously, the preciousness of a gold pendant with the "vegetable" (that is, "growing," "living") flesh of "real" fruit.

"Blooming," in the lines just quoted, is not the only noteworthy verbal form in this first description of Eden. The "verdurous wall" of Eden "*springs*" up (IV. 143). The sun "*impresses*" its beams on the fruit (IV. 150), and with sharp, almost solid, heat "*smites*" (IV. 244) the open fields. Nature "*pours* forth" her flowers (IV. 243), and the "mantling vine/*Lays forth* her purple grape, and gently *creeps*/ Luxuriant" (IV. 258–60). The streams, ministering to the needs of the plants "*visit*" them (IV. 240) with nectar. The gales "from their wings/*Flung* rose, *flung* odours from the spicy shrub" (VIII. 516–7). Perhaps most beautifully of all

> gentle gales
> Fanning their odoriferous wings dispense
> Native perfumes, and whisper whence they stole
> Those balmy spoils.
>
> (IV. 156–9)

The winds, momentarily semi-metamorphosed into delicate insects or birds, are imagined as engaged in a delighted, beneficent conspiracy to waft the sweet scents of wild flowers ("native perfumes") where they can best be relished. The sensuous sound effects of such lines are surely enough by themselves to refute F. R. Leavis's description of Milton's portrayal of Eden as "laboured pedantic artifice," and his assertion that Milton's grand style is incapable of displaying the "interest in sensuous particularity" to be found in the poetry of Keats.

The sounds of Paradise, in Milton's rendering, are as entrancing as its smells. Indeed, both are as one:

> The birds their choir apply; airs, vernal airs,
> Breathing the smell of field and grove, attune
> The trembling leaves, while universal Pan
> Knit with the Graces and the Hours in dance
> Led on the eternal Spring.
>
> (IV. 264–8)

"The airs attune the leaves," wrote William Empson, "because the air itself is as enlivening as an air [i.e. tune]; the trees and wild flowers that are smelt on the air match, as if they caused, as if they were caused by, the birds and leaves that are heard on the air; nature, because of a pun, becomes a single organism."[7]

The same delightful and delighted animism that informs the descriptions of Eden is evident in the evocations of creation, where we are also made to feel the goodness of a God who invests the things which He has made with a vigorous, spontaneous, independent life, in which He, and we, rejoice. Here, for example, is Milton's account of the creation of dry land:

> God said
> Be gathered now ye waters under Heaven
> Into one place, and let dry land appear.
> Immediately the mountains huge appear
> Emergent, and their broad bare backs upheave
> Into the clouds, their tops ascend the sky.
>
> (VII. 282–7)

The vast energy and solid bulk of the emerging mountains is vividly rendered by Milton's "upheave," which, placed as it is just before the line break, seems to mimic their surging rise from the ocean. The mountains' "broad bare backs" are at once the backs of enormous leviathans emerging from the sea and solid expanses of broad, hard rock. The effect is counterpointed by the more delicate and sensuous quality of the newly created vegetation, beautifully evoked in the verbal detail of Milton's description which, again, seems to imitate some of the textures which it describes:

> He scarce had said, when the bare earth, till then
> Desert and bare, unsightly, unadorned,
> Brought forth the tender grass, whose verdure clad
> Her universal face with pleasant green,
> Then herbs of every leaf, that sudden flowered
> Opening their various colours, and made gay
> Her bosom smelling sweet: and these scarce blown,
> Forth flourished thick the clustering vine, forth crept
> The swelling gourd, up stood the corny reed
> Embattled in her field; and the humble shrub,
> And bush, with frizzled hair implicit [tangled].
> (VII. 313–23)

Nature is seen both as a landscape and a female presence of delighted potency. The witty analogies – reed beds like hosts of extended spears (but so unlike those wielded by the fallen angels), bushes like unkempt heads of hair – are Milton's humorous poetic means of giving us fresh eyes to see and relish the miraculous nature of this newborn world.

Adam and Eve in Eden

Milton's Edenic Nature is at its most radiantly lovely, and most perfectly about its proper business, when celebrating the human inhabitants of the garden, and, in particular, the gloriously unashamed sexuality, the "mutual love" which, in sharp contrast to most of the earlier accounts of Edenic life known to Milton, is the "crown" of their "enormous bliss" (IV. 727; V. 297). Here Adam and Eve are entering for the night into their bower, the textures and movements of whose very vegetation seems to honor their coming:

> Thus talking hand in hand alone they passed
> On to their blissful bower; it was a place
> Chos'n by the sovereign planter, when he framed
> All things to man's delightful use; the roof
> Of thickest covert was inwoven shade
> Laurel and myrtle, and what higher grew
> Of firm and fragrant leaf; on either side
> Acanthus, and each odorous bushy shrub
> Fenced up the verdant wall; each beauteous flower
> Iris all hues, roses and jessamin
> Reared high their flourished heads between, and wrought
> Mosaic.
>
> (IV. 689–700)

The life which Adam and Eve enjoy together is founded and centered on perpetual pleasure, but a pleasure which is no mere shallow hedonism. Their labor on the luxurious garden is continuously punctuated, as Adam points out, with:

> Refreshment, whether food, or talk between,
> Food of the mind, or this sweet intercourse
> Of looks and smiles; for smiles from reason flow,
> To brute denied, and are of love the food;
> Love, not the lowest end of human life.
> For not to irksome toil, but to delight,
> He made us, and delight to reason joined.
>
> (IX. 237–43)

Their world, as these words of Adam's imply, is one in which there is no tension between body and soul, flesh and spirit, feeling and thought, action and reflection. As Raphael explains (V. 468–505), the Edenic world forms a continuous process in which matter and spirit pass into one another without any break or dislocation:

> So from the root
> Springs lighter the green stalk, from thence the leaves
> More airy, last the bright consummate flower
> Spirits odorous breathes; flowers and their fruit,
> Man's nourishment, by gradual scale sublimed
> To vital spirits aspire, to animal,
> To intellectual, give both life and sense,
> Fancy and understanding, whence the soul
> Reason receives, and Reason is her being.
>
> (V. 479–87)

There is an unbroken continuity in Paradise between the various elements: the earth which feeds the plant, the tender but vigorous stalk which supports the weightier flower which brings joy to the human senses (the contrast between the two is beautifully conveyed in Milton's "consummate"), and the fruit which feeds the human body and brain. Adam and Eve suffer from no "dissociation of sensibility."[8] Their "rational" thinking is, at one and the same time, acutely sensitive and delicate feeling. Adam's first "thoughts" when new-created (VIII. 253–69) derive directly from the acute pleasure which he feels in the appearance and workings of his own new-found body. There is no contradiction in this world between the earthy but entirely ungreedy relish with which Adam and Eve's eating is evoked –

> The savoury pulp they chew, and in the rind
> Still as they thirsted scoop the brimming stream.
>
> (IV. 335–6)

– and the radiantly lofty purity and majesty of their glorious appearance:

> Two of far nobler shape, erect and tall,
> Godlike erect, with native honour clad
> In naked majesty seemed lords of all,
> And worthy seemed, for in their looks divine
> The image of their glorious maker shone,

> Truth, wisdom, sanctitude severe and pure,
> Severe, but in true filial freedom placed,
> Whence true authority in men.
>
> (IV. 287–94)

The nakedness of their bodies is made, in Milton's poetic treatment, to symbolize their openness to the whole universe that lies around them. Milton, to quote A. J. Smith again, "has them attest for themselves the universal beneficence which surrounds them, showing us that they understand the harmony of which they are part, and acknowledge the bond between the human world and the universe of spirits."[9]

Adam and Eve are given long, formal poetic discourses, noticeably different in manner from each other's and from the voice of the poem's main narrator. Their speeches impress upon us the distinctive strengths of both. Adam's "poetry," though by no means lacking in sensuality, tends towards the calmly philosophical, and is impressive for its presentation of grand general principles in a manner which is, however, entirely lacking in pompous grandiloquence. Here he is, inviting Eve to retire for the night, and expounding, with orderly dignity, the benign significance in what, to a non-human observer, might seem the merely arbitrary and meaningless alternation of day and night. Adam's speech displays that very self-knowledge, that self-conscious awareness of the distinctiveness of his own species, which we are told (VII. 508–10) marked out man at his creation from other creatures and constituted his right to "govern" them:

> Fair consort, the hour
> Of night, and all things now retired to rest
> Mind us of like repose; since God hath set
> Labour and rest, as day and night, to men
> Successive, and the timely dew of sleep,
> Now falling with soft slumb'rous weight, inclines
> Our eyelids. Other creatures all day long
> Rove idle, unemployed, and less need rest;
> Man hath his daily work of body or mind
> Appointed, which declares his dignity,
> And the regard of Heaven on all his ways.
>
> (IV. 610–20)

Eve's beautifully shaped reply is one of the supreme poetic moments
of *Paradise Lost*:

> With thee conversing, I forget all time,
> All seasons and their change; all please alike.
> Sweet is the breath of morn, her rising sweet,
> With charm of earliest birds; pleasant the sun,
> When first on this delightful land he spreads
> His orient beams, on herb, tree, fruit, and flower,
> Glistering with dew; fragrant the fertile earth
> After soft showers; and sweet the coming on
> Of grateful evening mild; then silent night,
> With this her solemn bird, and this fair moon,
> And these the gems of heaven, her starry train;
> But neither breath of morn, when she ascends
> With charm of earliest birds; nor rising sun
> On this delightful land; nor herb, fruit, flower,
> Glistering with dew; nor fragrance after showers;
> Nor grateful evening mild; nor silent night,
> With this her solemn bird; nor walk by moon,
> Or glittering starlight, without thee is sweet.
>
> (IV. 639–56)

Eve's "poem" manifests consummate rhetorical mastery as it moves,
in one, enormous, effortlessly controlled breath, running through
the natural delights of a day in Eden to close on that which consti-
tutes the center of her bliss: her love for Adam. Her words are, at
one and the same time, religious poem, nature poem, and love
poem, for her apprehensions of nature are inseparable from her
feelings for God and for her husband. The word on which the
whole speech turns, and to which its formal movement constantly
recurs – "sweet" – is a potent one for Milton, signifying not only
exquisitely fragrant perfume but the deep contentment that comes
from feeling at one with a dispensation that ensures a perpetual joy
and a perpetual absence of the frustration, alienation and perplexity
which have been embodied for Adam and Eve in the tortured figures of the fallen angels. In Chapter 2 we saw how Adam, in Book
VIII, thanks Raphael for having taught him

                                                    to live
                    The easiest way, nor with perplexing thoughts
                    To interrupt the sweet of life, from which
                    God hath bid dwell far off all anxious cares.
                                                    (VIII. 182–5)

"The sweet of life" here stands for all that Adam and Eve enjoy
together in Eden. Their paradisal "conversations" do, indeed, lack
many of the characteristics we associate with the term in the postlapsarian world. Their exchanges are never – as ours so often are – at
cross purposes. There is never any will to dominate by either party.
Adam and Eve's dialogues can perhaps be thought of as the succes-
sive verses of a continuous hymn, in which, in their complementary
ways, each is concerned to find the best way to express their won-
dering delight at the miraculous world in which they have found
themselves. Their energies are entirely devoted to understanding –
an understanding at once sensual and intellectual – rather than to
disputation. Again, Coleridge offers one of the best accounts of
Milton's conception:

> The love of Adam and Eve in Paradise is of the highest merit – not
> phantomatic [purely "spiritual"], and yet removed from everything
> degrading. It is the sentiment of one rational being towards another
> made tender by a specific difference in that which is essentially
> the same in both; it is a union of opposites, a giving and receiving
> mutually of the permanent in either, a completion of each in the
> other.[10]

When considering Milton's depiction of Eden, one should always
remember how short a time the poet imagines Adam and Eve's life
in the garden to have occupied. In his Longman edition, Alastair
Fowler includes a table summarizing, on the strength of clues provided within the text, the imagined time-scheme of *Paradise Lost*.
Fowler suggests that the total action of the poem comprises 33
days, with the creation of the world beginning on day 14, the creation of man occurring on day 19, and the Fall at noon on day 32.
Such calculations might seem a somewhat pedantic way of charting
a poetic action of such cosmic scope and grandeur, and should not,

perhaps, be taken too literally or applied too rigorously. But they are nevertheless valuable in reminding us that Adam and Eve's life in Eden, as the poem presents it, was very short-lived.

This brief Edenic existence as Milton conceived it, moreover, was far from the condition of stasis assumed by some commentators. It is presented in the poem, rather as a state of "radical growth and process, a mode of life steadily increasing in complexity and challenge and difficulty but at the same time and by that very fact, in perfection."[11] Eden, in Milton's depiction is copiously fertile, and thus requires constant "cultivation." Raphael explicitly tells Adam and Eve (V. 388–91) that their "society" is destined to be increased and transformed by the procreation of children. Their discourses with the angel are shown to represent only the first step on the long voyage of discovery and self-development on which they have embarked. Though Raphael, as we have seen, warns Adam of the dangers of seeking the wrong kind of knowledge, in other respects he encourages Adam's exploratory questing to the full. Life in Eden is imagined, not as a state of bland inertia, but as dynamic, progressive, and exploratory.

Eve and the Relations between the Sexes

But as noted in Chapter 1, there is an aspect of Milton's depiction of prelapsarian life that, for some modern readers, presents an obstacle to the appreciation of *Paradise Lost* as serious as the embarrassment about Old Testament myth which so inhibited Victorian and post-Victorian responses to the poem.

Some modern commentators have argued that the hierarchically structured world of *Paradise Lost* has served to reinforce a radically conservative myth about the relations between the sexes. Everything female in *Paradise Lost*, such critics have suggested, is treated as suspect or inferior.[12] The Godhead is presented as exclusively male. Eve is created as an afterthought, and displays her narcissism immediately after her creation by admiring her own reflection in a pool. A secret kinship is implied between her and both Sin (the "only mother in the poem") and Satan, to whom she is sexually attracted: Eve's "rebelliousness" is deplored by the poet, on the assumption that disaster will inevitably ensue whenever Woman deviates from her divinely appointed role of serving Man. Creativity, except in the one sphere of maternal procreation, it has been said, is presented by Milton as a largely male preserve. Eve is portrayed as intellectually inferior to Adam, and is excluded from his dialogues with the angel. She is shown to fall by virtue of the vanity and susceptibility to flattery which have been characteristics of her nature from the start. Milton's narrative, such critics have suggested, was deeply contaminated with patriarchal assumptions which are not only unacceptable in themselves, but which have been catastrophic in their effects.

Feminist critics sympathetic to Milton have, however, vigorously contested such charges, arguing that they rest at each point on distinctly questionable interpretations of Milton's text.[13] It has been pointed out, for example, that Eve is not, in fact, absent during the bulk of Adam's conversations with Raphael, but hears the whole account of the angels' revolt and creation. When she does leave, at the beginning of Book VIII, Milton tells us quite specifically that this is *not* because she is intellectually incapable of understanding Adam's discourse with Raphael about the planetary motions, but because she prefers to hear such matters from Adam, whose less austere, but no less complete, mode of exposition she finds more congenial:

> Yet went she not, as not with such discourse
> Delighted, or not capable her ear
> Of what was high: such pleasure she reserved,
> Adam relating, she sole auditress;
> Her husband the relater she preferred
> Before the angel, and of him to ask
> Chose rather; he, she knew would intermix
> Grateful digressions, and solve high dispute
> With conjugal caresses, from his lip
> Not words alone pleased her.
>
> (VIII. 48–57)

Eve, we might say, prefers intellectual discourse which is not merely abstract, but grounded in a fully human context. Her sentiments are, indeed, strikingly similar in some respects to those which

Milton himself had earlier advocated in his own voice in the marriage tract, *Tetrachordon* (1645):

> We cannot ... always be contemplative, or pragmatical abroad, but have need of some delightful intermissions, wherein the enlarged soul may leave off a while her severe schooling, and, like a glad youth in wandering vacancy, may keep her holidays in joy and harmless pastime; which as she cannot well do without company, so in no company so well as where the different sex in most resembling unlikeness, and most unlike resemblance, cannot but please best, and be pleased in the aptitude of that variety.

It has, moreover, been pointed out that *Paradise Lost* teems with images of female creativity of all kinds. The perverted, incestuous sexuality of Sin, it has been argued, is offered precisely as a diabolical contrast to the sexuality of Eve, rather than as any kind of shadow or parallel. Eve's "submissiveness" to Adam, moreover, is no mere subservience. It is only *after* the Fall (X. 195–6) that Eve is subjected to Adam's will. Before that, she has no obligation to follow his commands if they do not accord with the findings of her own reason. The precise nature of the hierarchical relationship between Adam and Eve, Milton's admirers remind us, can only be properly understood within the very particular structure of hierarchies that exists in the poem. It cannot be simply transported and used as any kind of blueprint or model for behavior elsewhere. Furthermore, it has been argued, the charges that Eve is "narcissistic," that she falls because of gross and blatant intellectual deficiencies, or because of her ready susceptibility to Satan's flatteries, are directly contradicted in the relevant portions of Milton's text. We return to that point in Chapter 4.

Adam's Dialogue with Raphael

The controversies summarized above are relevant to a crucial passage in *Paradise Lost*, a brief discussion of which will provide an appropriate coda to this chapter. Towards the end of Book VIII, Adam is telling Raphael about the creation of Eve. He knows, because he has been told by the angel and by God, that Eve is, in some sense, supposed to be his "inferior, in the mind/And inward faculties, which most excel" (VIII. 541–2). But he cannot feel it that way:

> when I approach
> Her loveliness, so absolute she seems
> And in herself complete, so well to know
> Her own, that what she wills to do or say,
> Seems wisest, virtuousest, discreetest, best:
> All higher knowledge in her presence falls
> Degraded. Wisdom in discourse with her
> Loses discountenanced, and like folly shows;
> Authority and Reason on her wait,
> As one intended first, not after made
> Occasionally; and to consummate all,
> Greatness of mind and nobleness their seat
> Build in her loveliest, and create an awe
> About her, as a guard angelic placed.
>
> (VIII. 547–59)

Raphael warns Adam not to place too much credit in Eve's "outside," and not to be so swayed by his passion that he abdicates his position as Eve's "head." Adam comes boldly back at the angel. Raphael, he says, has seriously misunderstood him. He is not merely responding to Eve's physical beauty. Nor is his passion mere carnal pleasure, such as is felt by the beasts: the conjugal sexuality which he and Eve enjoy, is, in any case, quite unlike the mating of animals. What most impresses him about Eve, he insists, are:

> those graceful acts,
> Those thousand decencies that daily flow
> From all her words and actions, mixed with love
> And sweet compliance, which declare unfeigned
> Union of mind, or in us both one soul;
> Harmony to behold in wedded pair
> More grateful than harmonious sound to the ear.
>
> (VIII. 600–6)

Adam's word "decencies," as Patrick Hume, Milton's first annotator (1695) pointed out, exploits the Latin root of the English word (*decens*: comely, becoming) to evoke, beautifully the inextricability of Eve's sexual loveliness from the gracefulness of her daily actions and conduct.

Some commentators on this passage have assumed that Raphael is to be seen here as Milton's mouthpiece, issuing an ominous warning against the "uxoriousness" that will eventually be Adam's downfall. Others have responded so sympathetically to Adam's sentiments that they have seen a conflict between what Milton intends (Adam is to be disapproved of) and the effect of his passage on the reader (Adam is right, and we warm to his words).

But are these the only options? There is, surely, another possibility. Milton does indeed invite us to weigh the angel's warning. Adam must maintain a constant vigilance to ensure that he exercises his proper responsibilities within God's scheme. But the poet also gives powerful weight to Adam's responses. Adam acknowledges that Eve was, indeed, made "occasionally" (i.e. second), and for him, and that he has been told that she is, in some sense, to be thought less Godlike "in the mind/And inward faculties" (VIII. 541–2) and less "commanding" in her physical form. But, speaking with the full weight of his God-given eloquence and passionate reasonableness, in some of what is surely some of the most conspicuously beautiful verse in the whole poem – and some of the most gloriously uncondescending love poetry in the whole English language – he also affirms that he cannot, in her presence, *believe* these things to be so. When with Eve, Adam proclaims, he simply cannot think her inferior to him in any respect. Indeed, she seems superior: more perfect in both body and mind. These are, he insists, not merely irrational feelings. They are confirmed by his thinking and reflecting mind – the very thinking and reflective mind which marks out humankind as the culminating glory of God's creation. It is notable that Joseph Addison, from whom a moralistic rebuke might perhaps have been expected at this moment, responded to Adam's words with appreciative warmth:

> [Adam's] discourse, which follows the gentle rebuke he received from the angel, shows that his love, however violent it might appear, was still founded in reason, and consequently not improper for Paradise.

In an influential work, the Russian philosopher and literary theo-
rist Mikhail Bahktin famously suggested that while novels are "dialogic," containing a plurality of voices, none of which can be taken to
articulate the whole truth, the epic is monovocal, with the narrator's
voice occupying a position of unique, privileged authority, and with
all other voices in the poem being effectively those of puppets under
the narrator's control.[14] The dialogue between Adam and Raphael
which we have been considering points, I think, in a very different
direction. In a fine essay on the role of the narrator in *Paradise Lost*,
Fred Parker has suggested that it is unprofitable to adjudicate between
those (such as Alastair Fowler) who have insisted that the narrator's
voice in *Paradise Lost* is always to be taken as authoritative, and those
(such as Blake and Empson) who have seen the poem's action as
working *against* poet's own commentary. The difference in the poem
"between voice and event" should, Parker argues, be seen as "itself
part of the vital experience of *Paradise Lost*, and one whose satisfactions
depend precisely on its not being resolved in favour of either of the
parties."[15] In a similar vein, I would suggest that in a fully attentive
reading of the dialogue between Adam and Raphael we weigh the
words of both interlocutors, without simply siding with either. We
are both reminded of the vigilance which Adam and Eve must
maintain if they are to honor the responsibility and free will which
they have been given, while at the same being made aware of just
how difficult it will be for them to do that. The "meaning" of the
episode is not vested exclusively in either of the "voices" which speak,
but emerges from the totality of the exchange. It is thus with a sense
of the difficulties and complexities, rather than the mere error (or
admirableness) of Adam's position that we approach the events
leading to the Fall, which will be the subject of my final chapter.

Endnotes

1   Samuel Johnson, 'Life of Milton.'
2   E. M. W. Tillyard, *Milton* (revised edition, London, 1966), p. 239.
3   A strange remark, since it is the very first thing he does (VIII. 268).
4   *Coleridge on the Seventeenth Century*, p. 576.
5   A. J. Smith, *The Metaphysics of Love* (Cambridge, 1985), p. 23.

6   J. M. Newton, 'A Speculation About Landscape', *Cambridge Quarterly*, 4 (1969), 273–82 (pp. 273–4).

7   William Empson, *Some Versions of Pastoral* (London, 1935), p. 157.

8   T. S. Eliot's famous phrase for the hiving off of 'thought' from 'feeling' which, in his view 'set in' during the seventeenth century, and for which, in Eliot's view, Milton was partly responsible (see 'The Metaphysical Poets' (1921)).

9   *The Metaphysics of Love*, p. 120.

10   *Coleridge on the Seventeenth Century*, p. 579.

11   Barbara Kiefer Lewalski, 'Innocence and Experience in *Paradise Lost*', in Thomas Kranidas (ed.), *New Essays on Paradise Lost* (Berkeley LA and London, 1971), pp. 86–117 (p. 88).

12   In this paragraph, I draw mainly on the influential arguments of Sandra Gilbert and Susan Gubar, *The Madwoman in the Attic* (New Haven, 1979), and Marcia Landy, 'Kinship and the Role of Women in *Paradise Lost*', *Milton Studies*, 4 (1972), 3–18.

13   Here I draw principally on the arguments of Barbara K. Lewalski, 'Milton on Women – Yet Again', in *Problems for Feminist Criticism*, ed. Sally Minogue (London, 1990), pp. 46–69, and Diane Kelsey McColley, in *Milton's Eve* (Urbana, 1983).

14   See Mikhail Bakhtin, *The Dialogic Imagination*, trans. Caryl Emerson and Michael Holquist (Austin, 1982).

15   G. F. Parker, 'Marvell on Milton: Why the Poem Rhymes Not', *Cambridge Quarterly* (1991), 183–209 (p. 198).

4

The Fall

Milton, I have suggested, has prepared us for his presentation of the Fall by allowing us to experience both (in his depiction of Adam and Eve's life together in Eden) the beauties and pleasures of living according to God's law, and (in his depiction of Satan and the fallen angels) the alienation and despair that results from breaching that law. He has also impressed upon us the potential dangers, difficulties, and conflicting impulses that might be involved in maintaining obedience to God.

In this final chapter, I shall offer three main arguments. First, I shall suggest that Milton has handled the events leading up to the Fall with great delicacy and subtlety. The behavior of Eve, in particular, is handled with considerable tact, and Milton's portrayal has often been significantly coarsened by his commentators. Second, I shall suggest that, though we do not *admire* the conduct of Eve or Adam when they fall, we are given a very full and inward understanding of the steps that lead them to act in the way they do. Milton's main imaginative effort has gone in to explaining their action, and making it seem plausible. Apportionment of blame comes second to that, and the overall tone of Milton's portrayal of the Fall is more of sorrow than of anger. Third, I shall argue that because of what we have seen of Adam and Eve's Edenic life, we feel a great sense of loss ourselves at the moment of the Fall. But the poem does not end despairingly. The same God-given free will which has allowed Adam and Eve to fall in the first place allows them to pull themselves together after the

Reading Paradise Lost, First Edition. David Hopkins.
© 2013 John Wiley & Sons, Ltd. Published 2013 by John Wiley & Sons, Ltd.

disaster. 'All' is not, at the end of the poem, lost. *Paradise Lost* ends sadly, but on a note of muted hope rather than of despair.

Eve as Narcissus?

To read many commentaries on Book IX, one would think that Milton had portrayed Eve's actions in the scenes leading up to the Fall as merely selfish, vain, and gullible. A. W. Verity, in his edition of *Paradise Lost*, first published as long ago as the 1890s but much reprinted during the twentieth century, described Eve's conduct in a way that has found numerous echoes in later commentary:

> The picture [Milton] draws of Eve in this book is not agreeable. She is self-willed; easily flattered by the serpent; disobedient of command; selfish enough to drag Adam down in her fall; deceitful; and so mean-spirited as to reproach him.

Of Verity's remarks, I suggest that only those which apply to some of her conduct after the Fall have any real validity. The action of *Paradise Lost*, to be sure, is subtly shadowed at various moments by forebodings of the events to come – events which all readers of the poem will, of course, know in advance. Perhaps the most famous of such moments is the passage (IV. 268–86) in which the Garden of Eden is compared with the "fair field / Of Enna" in Sicily, where, according to Greek mythology, the goddess Proserpina was abducted by Pluto, god of the Underworld.[1] But such adumbrations of the Fall are subtly counterpointed in Milton's narration by equally powerful suggestions that until Eve's decision to eat the fruit, nothing occurs which will inevitably lead to catastrophe. Eve, it might be said, finally succumbs because of something that we might wish to call an intellectual lapse. But her behavior in the earlier parts of Book IX does not display simple weakness of understanding, or folly, let alone the grosser vices named by Verity. Milton, indeed, goes out of his way to make it clear that there is nothing sinful in Eve's departing to garden on her own, or in her listening to Satan's initial speeches of temptation. Throughout the scenes before her fall, she is shown to be exercising, perfectly properly, the free will and speculative powers which have been clearly established in the poem as two of God's greatest gifts to humankind.

One objection that is often made to Milton's handling of the coming of sin into the unfallen world is that since Adam and Eve had no experience of sin, they could have no real knowledge of what committing sin entails, and therefore could be in no real position to resist temptation. An unfair obligation, therefore, was put upon them by God, which they were in no real position to meet.[2]

It is true, of course, that Adam and Eve, before the Fall, have had no first-hand experience of sin, in that they have, as yet, committed no sinful act. But they have had a lengthy and graphic description of Satan's revolt, and of precisely what it means to willfully breach God's law. They also have a full and delighted sense of the bliss that they enjoy in Eden, and they know that to disobey God will be to lose Eden for ever. Moreover, it has been made clear in an important earlier episode in the poem that it is quite possible in the Edenic world, as Milton imagines it, to think and speculate about evil, to entertain thoughts of evil, to understand what evil entails, without being tainted by it. The episode is one in which, as in the Proserpina passage mentioned above, disturbing hints are offered as to what is to follow. But such hints are very far from prognostic certainties.

At the beginning of Book V, Eve has had a worrying dream. She has been tempted to eat the fruit of the Tree of Knowledge, has done so, and has experienced an extraordinary sensation of being lifted up to the clouds and being allowed to gaze down on the earth, miles beneath. In her dream, a voice has spoken to her and has suggested that Nature's nocturnal attention is devoted to her, and to her beauty:

> Now reigns
> Full orbed the moon, and with more pleasing light
> Shadowy sets off the face of things; in vain,
> If none regard; Heav'n wakes with all his eyes
> Whom to behold but thee, Nature's desire,
> In whose sight all things joy, with ravishment
> Attracted by thy beauty still to gaze.
>
> (V. 41–7)

The voice has seemed to supply a flattering answer to Eve's own earlier question about the purpose of the moon and starlight:

> But wherefore all night long shine these, for whom
> This glorious sight, when sleep hath shut all eyes?
> (IV. 657–8)

Eve awakes, troubled, and Adam consoles her with the thought that dreams are the mind's freewheeling, its working over, recombining, and distorting of fragments of previous experience and conversation without the governing, controlling, and censoring command of reason. Most of what Eve has dreamt, Adam goes on, can be explained as a wild distortion of their last night's conversation. There is, indeed, a sinister extra element present. But, Adam concludes, though they must be wary, there is no need for Eve to be perturbed, since

> Evil into the mind of God or man
> May come and go, so unapproved, and leave
> No spot or blame behind: which gives me hope
> That what in sleep thou did'st abhor to dream,
> Waking thou never wilt consent to do.
> (V. 117–21)

These words are significant since, though we certainly remember the dream incident with some concern during the scene describing Eve's temptation, some commentators would have us believe that Eve had already, in effect, fallen long before she actually eats the fruit. It is important to note that Milton explicitly describes her, after she has debated with Adam the advantages of going off alone, after she has had her first long exchange with the serpent, and after the serpent has led her to the Tree of Knowledge as "Eve, *yet sinless*" (IX. 659; my emphasis). We are, to be sure, fully cognizant of the dangers she faces, but as yet no sin has occurred.

It seems, however, that Milton has treated Eve so subtly, both in Book IX and earlier in the poem, that his drift was particularly prone to misrepresentation almost from the start. The following remark was included in a contributor's letter to No. 325 of *The Spectator*:

The design of this letter is to desire your thoughts whether there may not ... be some moral couched under that place in [*Paradise Lost*] where the poet lets us know that the first woman, immediately after her creation, ran to a looking-glass, and became so enamoured of her face that she had never removed to view any of the other works of Nature, had not she been led off to a man.

This comment was perhaps wittily intended. But, even if that is the case, the joke seems to rest on a gross travesty of the passage in the poem (IV. 440–86) to which it alludes. Eve's tone, as she remembers the events immediately after her creation, is humorously reflective. As she recalls seeing her own reflection in the lake, she wittily and amusedly mimics, in a manner reminiscent of the verbal repetitions characteristic of the Roman poet Ovid (one of Milton's favorite authors), her own remembered movements:

> As I bent down to look, just opposite
> A shape within the watery glass appeared,
> Bending to look on me: I started back,
> It started back; but pleased I soon returned,
> Pleased it returned as soon with answering looks
> Of sympathy and love.
>
> (IV. 460–5)

Eve's pleasure at her own appearance is no mere "narcissism." She *is*, after all, wonderfully beautiful. God himself refers to her, only a few lines later, as "fair creature" (IV. 469). But she does not, like Narcissus, in the episode from Ovid's *Metamorphoses* on which Milton here draws, remain pining "with vain desire" at her own image. She is led to Adam, who at first seems to her strangely forbidding, and nothing like as appealing as the beautiful image in the water, but with whom, eventually, she finds her deepest satisfaction. Her retelling of her own story is imbued with its teller's delicate and humorous self-awareness, and with the warmth of its occasion. It is a favorite story shared by two lovers who are blissfully at ease in one another's presence. Though the story of Narcissus, and its suggestions of self-absorption and self-love, subtly reminds us of the dangers of such feelings – feelings that will, indeed, play their part in Eve's eventual Fall – Milton's poem makes no simple identification of Eve with Narcissus. The classical story is recast in a prelapsarian context that entirely transforms it.

Something of the same general bias assumed in the *Spectator* contributor's comments on the "mirror" scene (quoted above) is found in some of the remarks of the commentators, from the eighteenth century to our own times, on Book IX. We will shortly examine some of the things they say about the discussion which Adam and Eve have about whether she should depart to garden alone. But before that, I offer a paraphrase-cum-commentary of my own which attempts to describe, as accurately as possible, the main drift of what happens in that dialogue. Readers will judge for themselves, when they compare what I say in detail with Milton's text, whether they think I have been fair to what I take to be the poet's main nuances and emphases.

The Conversation before Eve's Departure

Eve first approaches Adam (IX. 205). The vegetation of Eden, she suggests, is responding so well to their gardening that its lavish profusion is in danger of getting out of hand. Would it not, therefore, be better if, for a while, they were to garden separately, to prevent them from being distracted from performing their day's appointed tasks by dallying in "conversation"?

Adam approves what Eve says, and confirms that solitary contemplation is, indeed, sometimes desirable. Eve's motives, he realizes, are entirely admirable. She is trying to think of the best possible way of performing the work which God has assigned them. Yet their conversation should not be seen as a distraction, but, rather as that which gives a center, meaning, and purpose to all their other activities,

> For not to irksome toil, but to delight
> He made us, and delight to Reason joined.
> (IX. 242–3)

Moreover, as they have been warned, their tempter is near. If they garden separately, they are both making themselves more vulnerable to his wiles. The tempter would, however, be

> Hopeless to circumvent us joined, where each
> To other speedy aid might lend at need.
>
> (IX. 259–60)

In particular, Adam feels that it is his duty to protect his wife from any possible danger. It is, indeed, their conjugal love that Satan will envy more than anything else.

Eve replies to Adam's words. Her tone is sweet, calm and loving, yet she is concerned that her beloved Adam seems to be implying that she will succumb to temptation. She speaks

> As one who loves, and some unkindness meets,
> With sweet austere composure.
>
> (IX. 271–2)

Patrick Hume glossed "with sweet austere composure" as "in a more serious, yet sweet manner."

Adam replies once more. Eve, he realizes is, of course, free "from sin and blame entire" (IX. 292). It is not that he in any way mistrusts her. It is more that he does not want her to expose herself even to the possibility of temptation. He also needs her by him. Her presence would steady him in any momentary lapse of vigilance.

Eve again replies lovingly. They can suffer no harm, she says, unless they succumb. The only person to suffer from an attempt to corrupt them would be Satan, the tempter himself. If they were tempted and withstood, then they would be showing the real power of their God-given virtue.

Adam responds once again. His tone is concerned, but still loving. What she says is true. Yet man's will, if it is to remain pure, must always be subservient to his reason, and therein lies the danger, since it is possible that reason, unless it is perpetually vigilant, might misinterpret the evidence with which it is presented. They both, therefore, need the checking and steadying influence of one another's reason, to be sure that neither of them is being deceived. It would therefore be better if she stayed with him. Her loyalty to God would, in his view, be better displayed that way than by going off on her own; but if she genuinely feels that to go off would be the better course, then that is what she must do, for it would be wrong of him to command her to do something with which her own wishes were at variance.

Eve thanks Adam for his advice. Satan would, she says, surely not seek to triumph over humankind by seeking to corrupt *her*. So she will go. She leaves, and as she departs, she strikes Adam as more beautiful than the most radiant nymphs and goddesses of Greek myth.

Readers will, as I have said, judge for themselves whether that account is a fair representation of the sequence of events and sentiments as Milton presents them. But what I hope can be immediately agreed is that the following is certainly not acceptable as an account of the scene:

> The harmony of Paradise is broke by Eve's pride. She will not bear being advised, as implying some suspicion of her. The whole scene is admirably wrought up. The breach was occasioned by a trifle in appearance, and what seemed to have a right motive, a concern to do well – exceedingly plausible! But by insensible steps this little-suspected cause produced a melancholy effect which produced a much worse. They part, she triumphing in her obstinacy, and not content with his diffidence [= mistrustfulness] of her, and he as little pleased to find her not so perfect as he had imagined.

That, I am afraid to say, is the Jonathan Richardsons, usually so sensitive to Milton's meaning, but here (p. 409) displaying a coarse reductiveness which seriously misrepresents what happens during this stretch of dialogue. Robert Thyer, another eighteenth-century commentator, hardly fared better:

> With what strength is the superior excellency of man's understanding here pointed out, and how nicely does our author here sketch out the defects peculiar in general to the female mind!

But lest it should be supposed that such comments merely display a male bias only to be expected from eighteenth-century critics, let us consider for a moment the commentary on this section of the poem in Alastair Fowler's Longman edition.

"It is true," writes Fowler (a propos of Eve's proposal that she should go off and garden alone) "that, in so far as she argues about means without considering ends, Eve resembles, in a general way, the modern technocrat." Here are some of Eve's words at this moment, as Milton gives them:

> Let us divide our labours, thou where choice
> Leads thee, or where most needs, whether to wind
> The woodbine round this arbour, or direct the
> The clasping ivy where to climb, while I
> In yonder spring of roses intermixed
> With myrtle find what to re-dress till noon.
>
> (IX. 214–9)

On these lines, Fowler quotes with approval Christopher Ricks's comment: "Eve doesn't care what he does, and she knows very well what she will do." But this surely attributes to Eve a devious knowingness that goes far beyond anything warranted by Milton's text? A similar attribution of sinister psychological motives to Eve occurs in another of Fowler's notes, a few lines later. When Eve calls Adam "Offspring of heaven and earth" (273), Fowler comments: "Eve is now standing on her dignity." But Eve's words, are, surely, merely one of the stately forms of address which both Adam and Eve deploy throughout the poem (the forms of address which John Carey disliked because they "prohibit conversational interplay" in Eden)?

Like other commentators, Fowler sees similarities between some of the arguments employed by Eve and those which appear in a famous passage from *Areopagitica* (1644), Milton's prose pamphlet on censorship and freedom of the press:

> Good and evil we know in the field of this world grow up together almost inseparably; and the knowledge of good is so involved and interwoven with the knowledge of evil, and in so many cunning resemblances hardly to be discerned, that those confused seeds which were imposed upon Psyche as an incessant labour to cull out, and sort asunder, were not more intermixed. It was from out the rind of one apple tasted, that the knowledge of good and evil, as two twins cleaving together, leaped forth into the world. And perhaps this is that doom which Adam fell into of knowing good and evil, that is

to say of knowing good by evil. As therefore the state of man now is; what wisdom can there be to choose, what continence to forbear without the knowledge of evil? He that can apprehend and consider vice with all her baits and seeming pleasures, and yet abstain, and yet distinguish, and yet prefer that which is truly better, he is the true warfaring Christian.

I cannot praise a fugitive and cloistered virtue, unexercised and unbreathed, that never sallies out and sees her adversary but slinks out of the race, where that immortal garland is to be run for, not without dust and heat. Assuredly we bring not innocence into the world, we bring impurity much rather; that which purifies us is trial, and trial is by what is contrary. That virtue therefore which is but a youngling in the contemplation of evil, and knows not the utmost that vice promises to her followers, and rejects it, is but a blank virtue, not a pure; her whiteness is but an excremental whiteness.

Here, in immediate juxtaposition, are the relevant words of Eve:

> If this be our condition, thus to dwell
> In narrow circuit straightened by a foe,
> Subtle or violent, we not endued
> Single with like defence, wherever met,
> How are we happy, still in fear of harm?
> But harm precedes not sin: only our foe
> Tempting affronts us with his foul esteem
> Of our integrity: his foul esteem
> Sticks no dishonour on our front, but turns
> Foul on himself; then wherefore shunned or feared
> By us? who rather double honour gain
> From his surmise proved false, find peace within,
> Favour from Heaven, our witness from th' event.
> And what is Faith, Love, Virtue unassayed'
> Alone, without exterior help sustained?
> Let us not then suspect our happy state
> Left so imperfect by the Maker wise,
> As not secure to single or combined.
> Frail is our happiness, if this be so,
> And Eden were no Eden thus exposed.
>
> (IX. 322–41)

Fowler comments:

> We should not assume that because in *Areopagitica* Milton rejects
> "cloistered virtue" he therefore approves Eve's sentiments here, in
> the very different context of an unfallen world ... At the same time,
> Milton would naturally want to involve his own cherished convic-
> tions and aspirations in Eve's dangerous individualism; both for the
> sake of idealizing her, and in the interests of self-discovery.

Fowler suggests that Milton is both giving Eve arguments to which
he was personally committed, and simultaneously inviting us to see
how those arguments are invalid in a prelapsarian context. This
argument is in some ways similar to that (mentioned in Chapter 2)
by which Milton is shown to have given Satan republican sentiments close to his own, in order to expose Satan as a false republican. But has the general similarity of subject matter, together with
the explicit mention of Adam in the *Areopagitica* passage, encouraged Fowler and other commentators to conclude that its argument is closer to that of Eve's speech in *Paradise Lost* than it actually
is? The passage from *Areopagitica* seems to be making two main
points: first, that in the world we live in (the fallen world), virtue
and vice are sometimes virtually indistinguishable, and it is therefore the task of the true Christian to make fine distinctions, in order
to separate virtues from the vices that so closely resemble them;
second, that virtue is nothing unless it is tested. Eve's argument in
the poem, in contrast, surely goes more like this:

> How can we be called happy if we are so afraid of Satan that we do not
> dare to go off alone? We cannot come to any harm unless we sin. The
> only person to suffer if we are tempted will be the tempter himself,
> so is it not absurd of *us* to fear *him*? If we are tempted and resist, that
> will make our virtue seem all the more solid. We will be at peace, no
> longer troubled by the threat of Satan. And we will have shown God
> our merit. We cannot legitimately call ourselves "virtuous" if our vir-
> tue is entirely dependent on the protection of others. If God is good,
> we cannot be as weak as we now seem to be implying that we are.

That is surely a subtly different argument from that in *Areopagitica*,
and, moreover, a rather good one. Adam, at any rate, finds it very

difficult to answer. The fact that we are apprehensive because we know what will be the outcome of Eve's departure should not lead us to attribute to Milton a pejorative interpretation of Eve's sentiments ("dangerous individualism") which – or so I would argue – his text scrupulously avoids.

Eve as Goddess

At the moment of Eve's departure Milton makes rich and extensive use of parallels from Greek myth:

> Thus saying, from her husband's hand her hand
> Soft she withdrew, and like a wood-nymph light
> Oread or Dryad, or of Delia's train,
> Betook her to the groves, but Delia's self
> In gait surpassed and goddess-like deport,
> Though not as she with bow and quiver armed,
> But with such gardening tools as art yet rude,
> Guiltless of fire had formed, or angels brought.
> To Pales, or Pomona, thus adorned,
> Likeliest she seemed, Pomona when she fled
> Vertumnus, or to Ceres in her Prime,
> Yet Virgin of Proserpina from Jove.
>
> (IX. 385–96)

The eighteenth-century scholar Lord Monboddo described the reaction which he thought Milton was expecting from his readers at this moment:

As this is the last description of Eve in a state of innocence, Milton has bestowed upon her the richest colours of his poetry, and has compared her to every thing most beautiful of the kind that is to be found in ancient fable.

Another early commentator, Zachary Pearce, explained more precisely the connotations of each of Milton's mythological parallels:

She was likened to the wood-nymphs and Delia in regard to her gait [manner of walking, deportment]; but now that Milton had mentioned her being armed with garden tools, he beautifully compares her to Pales, Pomona, and Ceres, all three goddesses like to each other in these circumstances: that they were handsome, that they presided over gardening and cultivation of ground, and that they were usually described by the ancient poets as carrying tools of gardening or husbandry in their hands: ... Milton's meaning is that [Eve] was like Pomona, not precisely at the hour when she fled Vertumnus, but at the time of her life when Vertumnus made his addresses to her, that is when she was in all her perfection of beauty, as described by Ovid [in Book XIV of the *Metamorphoses*].

But Alastair Fowler sees a more sinister import in Milton's classical allusions:

The simile is so discriminating that it consists mainly of qualifications. Eve is like the immortal Diana (called Delia from Delos, her secluded island birthplace and refuge ...) but lacks the quiver of counsel .... Instead she has gardening tools .... Pomona might be thought a morally favourable analogue ... Milton, however, specifically refers to her seduction by the disguised Vertumnus.

Fowler's suggestion is that an alert contemporary reader would have noticed that Eve lacks Diana's "quiver of counsel." To support this suggestion, he cites the allegorical interpretation of Diana's quiver by Pierio Valeriano in his *Hieroglyphica*, a treatise on Egyptian hieroglyphics and other ancient religious rites published in Frankfurt in 1613. We know that Milton, like other learned Renaissance poets, knew many later interpretations of classical myth, as well as the retellings of the stories in the Greek and Roman poets themselves. He may well, therefore, have been acquainted with Valeriano's interpretation of Diana. But can we be certain that he was expecting readers to remember Valeriano's gloss rather than the more positive retellings of the myths in the poetic sources alluded to by Monboddo and Pearce? And should we necessarily suppose that the allusion to the story of Vertumnus and Pomona was chosen primarily because of its ominous similarity to the forthcoming "seduction" of Eve, rather than for the analogy between Eve's radiant loveliness to that of the beautiful Pomona?

If one remembers the story of Vertumnus and Pomona in Ovid's *Metamorphoses* one recalls that, far from being a sordid tale of deceitful rape, the fable is one which, though it involves disguise and deception in its earlier stages, culminates in happy, fulfilled love, with the country god Vertumnus revealing himself in all his youthful splendor to the rural goddess Pomona, who puts aside her earlier virginal reticence and joins him in glorious amatory bliss. Here is the culminating moment in Sir Samuel Garth's eighteenth-century translation:

> Like snow she melts; so soon can youth persuade;
> Consent, on eager wings, succeeds desire,
> And both the lovers glow with mutual fire.[3]

I have dwelt on these details in Fowler's commentary not to carp ungratefully at a distinguished scholar's work, but to suggest that apparently neutral presentations of scholarly data may sometimes contain interpretative suggestions which one might wish to question. More specifically, I wanted to use Fowler's commentary to throw into relief the degree to which Milton has depicted Eve's parting from Adam not as the willful action of a headstrong female but as a responsible act supported by reasonable arguments. While Adam is certainly not happy about them, and while we are, of course, apprehensive, since we know the story and thus know what the outcome will be, her actions are not presented as, in themselves, outrageous, absurd, stupid, or wicked. Nor is Adam's unhappiness any sort of sign that Paradise is, as some commentators have suggested, already lost at this point. Addison's general comment on the separation debate is worth remembering:

> The dispute ... between our first two parents is represented with great art. It proceeds from a difference of judgement, not of passion, and is managed with reason, not with heat. It is such a dispute as we may suppose might have happened in Paradise, had Man continued happy and innocent.

Our feelings as readers are exquisitely and vertiginously poised. We both respect Eve's sentiments, and share Adam's fears about their potential danger. The poignancy of the moment, as captured by Milton, is beautifully described by the Richardsons:

> His forced consent is finely marked. She drew away her hand from his, yet wishing to detain her, loath, dreading to part. In vain! 'tis a master-touch of tenderness in few words.

Eve's Temptation

The same bias that one can detect in commentaries on Eve's conduct before her departure can also be found in accounts of her temptation itself. Again, I think is it far from Milton's intention to suggest that Eve falls because of some (so to speak) "in-built" intellectual or moral weakness or flaw. Her conduct is portrayed, right to the last moment, in the most understanding light, with every effort being made by the poet to explain precisely how it was that she eventually yielded to temptation. Milton has exercised all his artistry on depicting Eve's spellbinding beauty and innocence as she gardens alone, and on portraying the effects (quoted in an earlier chapter) which the sight of her has on Satan, temporarily dumbfounding him and momentarily diverting him from his evil purpose. Satan's consummate persuasiveness is both displayed and authorially underlined throughout the temptation scenes. It is often said that Eve capitulates all too readily to arrant flattery on Satan's part. Flattery certainly plays its part in her collapse. But it is only one element. And to stress it at the expense of other relevant factors is to forget the canny skepticism which she displays after Satan's first speech:

> Serpent, thy overpraising leaves in doubt
> The virtue of that fruit, in the first proved.
> (IX. 615–6)

– which Patrick Hume paraphrased thus: "Thy extolling me so extremely makes me doubt of the wondrous power thou pretendest to have experienced in that tree, to raise and enlarge thy faculties to nobler speculations."

Milton seems, in fact, to have placed the main emphasis, when accounting for Eve's collapse, on the general persuasiveness of Satan's arguments rather than on his flattery or sexual seductiveness. The poet also included a number of touches in his retelling of the story which combine to make Eve's conduct far more understandable than it is in the Bible. The serpent in the Book of Genesis merely exhorts Eve to eat the fruit. Milton's serpent claims to have eaten it himself. On this point, Patrick Hume has a very perceptive note:

> Our poet has so finely handled the serpent's temptation as to answer all the allegations made of Eve's wonderful simplicity, etc. He introduceth the Devil, reasoning in the Serpent, to so strange a degree, pretending by his eating of the forbidden tree to have obtained both speech and reason, exalted and ennobled thereby above all other creatures, that the objections Pererius[4] puts into her mouth would have been no defence to her: "The woman said to the serpent, 'If things are indeed as you have said, why don't you eat from that tree, so that you can admire for yourself the things you have promised me? Go on, you eat first, so that I can test out whether these thing you are telling me and promising me are true.'"

Even circumstances, in Milton's telling, conspire to make Eve's fall more likely:

> Meanwhile the hour of noon drew on, and waked
> An eager appetite, raised by the smell
> So savoury of that fruit, which with desire
> Inclinable now grown to touch or taste
> Solicited her longing eye.
>
> (IX. 739–43)

Thomas Newton commented: "This is a circumstance beautifully added by our author to the Scripture account, in order to make the folly and impiety of Eve appear less extravagant and monstrous." Because of such touches, when the poet writes that Satan's words "replete with guile / Into her heart too easy entrance won" (IX. 733–4), we cannot, I think, take "too easy" as mere condescension.

The narrator's comment is made as much in horror, sadness, and lament as in censorious disapproval.

Milton, as already mentioned, provides a crucial marker when he describes Eve, as she arrives with Satan at the Tree of Knowledge, as "yet sinless" (IX. 659). Nothing that Eve has yet said or done has been sinful, nor have any of her actions been irrevocable. But once Eve stops by the Tree of Knowledge to listen to Satan, who now (IX. 664–78) pulls out extra stops of rhetorical persuasiveness, she is putting an intolerable strain on the reason which she knows, and which Adam has confirmed, can certainly be deceived by specious evidence. "Eve 'falls,'" as Jean Gooder notes, "precisely as evil enters her head unchecked." She approves what lies "within her power to resist." Her "wilful crime," as she later calls it (XII. 619), is to have allowed herself to be misinformed and deceived, so that "what God had expressly forbidden" seems to her to be actually "recommended" by her Reason.[5] As she is persuaded by Satan's words, she convinces herself that eating the fruit will not bring death, since the serpent still lives. Eating the fruit, she supposes, will bring the knowledge that will make clear what seem at present unfathomable mysteries. As she eats, Milton's presentation underlines the appalling moment of loss, as the Nature with whom Adam and Eve have hitherto lived in such intimate harmony is convulsed at her action:

> Earth felt the wound, and Nature from her seat
> Sighing through all her works gave signs of woe
> That all was lost.
>
> (IX. 782–4)

Though we have seen her teetering ever more precariously towards the brink, it is, of course, the *act* of eating itself, the physical expression of the conscious decision to go against God's law, the transformation of speculation into deed – a fine distinction, potently symbolized by the apparently trivial action of eating a fruit – that is decisive. The knowledge that first Eve, then Adam, acquire by eating is quite different from the godlike delights which Satan has promised. It is, rather, the agonizing consciousness of having cut themselves off from that intimate rapport with themselves, each other, their creator, and their surroundings, which they have enjoyed in Eden. We see the change immediately. As Eve eats, her former vigorous chewing (IV. 335) becomes greedy "engorging," "without restraint" (IX. 791). She begins to take a view of God similar to that of William Empson, seeing Him as a prying, devious tyrant. She becomes anxious about her capacity to attract Adam, then consumed with the desire to dominate him, mouthing sentiments with which we are familiar from Satan: "for inferior, who is free?" (IX. 825)

Adam's Fall

As Eve returns to Adam, he, aghast at what has happened, resolves to join her in her fallen state. Adam does not share the illusion that the knowledge he will acquire will be wonderful and godlike. But, for him, with the Fall of his beloved Eve, Eden has already, in effect, been lost. Virtually all readers of the poem, including some of Milton's harshest critics, acknowledge that this is a powerfully moving moment, and that Adam is here given some wonderfully convincing dramatic verse, in which, despite – or because – of its studied repetitions and alliteration, we seem to be given direct and intimate access to the deepest regions of his thoughts and emotions:

> O fairest of creation, last and best
> Of all God's works, creature in whom excelled
> Whatever can to sight or thought be formed,
> Holy, divine, good, amiable, or sweet!
> How art thou lost! how on a sudden lost,
> Defaced, deflowered, and now to death devote!
> Rather, how hast thou yielded to transgress
> The strict forbiddance, how to violate
> The sacred fruit forbidden! Some cursed fraud
> Of enemy hath beguiled thee, yet unknown,
> And me with thee hath ruined; for with thee
> Certain my resolution is to die:
> How can I live without thee! how forego
> Thy sweet converse, and love so dearly joined,

To live again in these wild woods forlorn!
Should God create another Eve, and I
Another rib afford, yet loss of thee
Would never from my heart; no, no, I feel
The link of Nature draw me: flesh of flesh,
Bone of my bone thou art, and from thy state
Mine never shall be parted, bliss or woe.

(IX. 896–916)

Adam expresses his horror at Eve's "bold deed" (IX. 921). God, he reflects, surely would not destroy his favored creatures? Whatever the outcome, Adam's destiny, he declares, must lie with Eve:

However I with thee have fixed my lot,
Certain to undergo like doom: If death
Consort with thee, death is to me as life;
So forcible within my heart I feel
The bond of Nature draw me to my own;
My own in thee, for what thou art is mine;
Our state cannot be severed; we are one,
One flesh; to lose thee were to lose myself.

(IX. 952–9)

A. J. A. Waldock thought that our sympathies at this point are too wholeheartedly with Adam for the good of Milton's narrative logic. So moved are we, he argued, by Adam's affirmation of his love for Eve that we are not really convinced, despite Milton's authorial commentary, that what he is doing is so momentously terrible. We value his expression of love far more than we lament the loss of anything that it might be violating. Other, more pious, commentators have argued the opposite: that we should withhold our sympathies from Adam altogether, merely concentrating on the enormity and wickedness of his deed. But to take either of these extreme views is, I would suggest, to squint at Milton's text with one or other eye firmly and unresponsively closed. The poet's moving lines surely require us both to feel intimate and inward sympathy with Adam's plight *and* to share with him a powerful and appalled sense of precisely what they will be losing in sacrificing all that Eden has embodied. In the manner described by Fred Parker in the passage quoted at the end of Chapter 3, Milton's authorial commentary, in which we are told that Adam is "fondly overcome with female charm" (IX. 999), complements, and acts in tension with, rather than merely contradicts, his dramatic presentation.

Adam eats, and joins Eve in her fallen state. The world which they now inhabit is very different from the harmonious existence they have known hitherto. It is a world where aspiration and attainment are at odds, where body is, for the first time, at war with soul, where reason is at loggerheads with the senses. Their sexual life becomes heated appetite, a matter of consciously savoring their desires rather than expressing and celebrating them directly with uninhibited, spontaneous relish. They are now ashamed of their own bodies. Their eating is gluttonous. Their bodily and mental functions are disordered, troubled, and disturbed. They try to blame one another for their actions. They know mortality and fear of death for the first time. Their minds are constantly "perplexed" with "anxious cares." The "sweet of life" has been lost. Samuel Johnson described their new state thus:

> With guilt enter distrust and discord, mutual accusation and stubborn self-defence; they regard each other with alienated minds, and dread their creator as the avenger of their transgression.

Their new-found knowledge is indeed, as God later says, "knowledge of good lost and evil got" (XI. 87).

After the Fall

Paradise Lost, however, does not end with the Fall, and though there is only space for the most cursory glance at the last three books of the poem, one cannot underestimate their importance in establishing the balance of thoughts and feelings with which *Paradise Lost* finally leaves us about God's ultimate goodness to humanity.

If it is by exercising their God-given free will that Adam and Eve fall in the first place, it is by the exercise of precisely the same faculty that they pull themselves back slowly and painfully from the brink of suicide, and resolve to make something of their lives, even when their former bliss seems to have utterly collapsed. If their paradisal mutuality can never be recalled in its former, pure, state, it is by their mutual aid that Adam and Eve (with Eve, significantly, often taking the leading role) are able to resist the despair that could so easily have overcome them after their initial realization. Despite the horrifying entry of Sin and Death into the world via a bridge from Hell across Chaos (memorably described in Book X), and despite the sober revelation of future human sin and calamity – from the Flood to the Last Judgment – which Michael offers in Books XI and XII, Adam and Eve are consoled by the hope which they are offered of the Son's incarnation and resurrection. Even when their pride and dignity are sadly diminished after the Fall, it is still, as Johnson noted, "not [as] mean suitors" that they beg for God's mercy. To the very end of the poem, they still, even in their fallen state, preserve many of the essential attributes of God's chosen creatures. Paradise is lost, but a surprising amount of it is still, as Michael tells them, recoverable, albeit fitfully and momentarily:

> This having learned, thou hast attained the sum
> Of wisdom; hope no higher, though all the stars
> Thou knew'st by name, and all the ethereal powers,
> All secrets of the deep, all Nature's works,
> Or works of God in heav'n, air, earth, or sea,
> And all the riches of this world enjoyed'st,
> And all the rule, one empire; only add
> Deeds to thy knowledge answerable; add faith,
> Add virtue, patience, temperance; add love,
> By name to come called charity, the soul
> Of all the rest: then wilt thou not be loath
> To leave this Paradise, but shalt possess
> A Paradise within thee, happier far.
>
> (XII. 575–87)

As the poem ends, Adam and Eve are certainly much saddened, but their tears on leaving Paradise do not persist. As they depart from Eden for the last time, the world that is "all before them" offers opportunity as well as uncertainty and, though their gait is sober and faltering, they are once more, we note, hand in hand:

> They, looking back, all the eastern side beheld
> Of Paradise, so late their happy seat,
> Waved over by that flaming brand; the gate
> With dreadful faces thronged, and fiery arms:
> Some natural tears they dropped, but wiped them soon;
> The world was all before them where to choose
> Their place of rest, and Providence their guide:
> They, hand in hand, with wandering steps and slow,
> Through Eden took their solitary way.
>
> (XII. 641–9)

Endnotes

1   For a full and sensitive reading of this passage and its significance, see Charles Martindale, *John Milton and the Transformation of Ancient Epic* (London, 1986), pp. 171–81.

2   For a recent version of this argument, see Christopher Tilmouth's essay in Paul Hammond and Blair Worden (eds), *John Milton: Life, Writing, Reputation* (Oxford, 2010).

3   *Ovid's Metamorphoses, in Fifteen Books, Translated by the Most Eminent Hands* (London, 1717), p. 504.

4   Benedict Pereira (1535–1610), a Spanish Jesuit commentator on Genesis. Hume gives his words, which I have here translated, in Latin.

5   Jean Gooder, '"Fixt Fate" and "Free Will" in *Phèdre and Macbeth*', *Cambridge Quarterly*, 28 (1999), 214–31 (p. 217).

Further Reading

Commentary on *Paradise Lost* is vast. The following suggestions make no attempt at comprehensiveness, but are merely designed to indicate some useful, stimulating, and accessible starting points (many of which themselves have suggestions for further reading) for those wishing to explore some of the matters discussed in the present book, and others for which there was no room in a book of this size.

Editions

Paradise Lost is probably best first encountered in an edition that provides sufficiently full explanation of linguistic difficulties and references in Milton's text, without burdening the reader prematurely with too much ancillary learning. The best option is now probably the old-spelling edition by Barbara K. Lewalski (Oxford, 2007), which has on-the-page glossing and annotation, and an excellent Introduction. An alternative is John Leonard's Penguin Classics edition (revised, Harmondsworth, 2003) which is in modernized spelling, with notes at the back. Dennis Danielson's *Paradise Lost by John Milton: Parallel Prose Edition* (Vancouver, 2008) offers a complete *en face* prose paraphrase of the poem, which can sometimes help in unravelling Milton's more complex syntactical effects. Both beginners and more experienced readers will greatly benefit from hearing the poem read aloud. There is an

Reading Paradise Lost, First Edition. David Hopkins.
© 2013 John Wiley & Sons, Ltd. Published 2013 by John Wiley & Sons, Ltd.

excellent complete recording of the poem by Anton Lesser on Naxos Audiobooks (9 CDs: NA935012).

The early commentaries on the poem by Patrick Hume (1695), Zachary Pearce (1732), Jonathan Richardson, father and son (1734), Thomas Newton (1749) and H. J. Todd (1801) contain much sensitive close attention to Milton's meanings and sources, and are still well worth consulting on particular points and passages. Hitherto only available in major libraries, and so effectively inaccessible to ordinary readers, the late seventeenth- and eighteenth-century commentaries are now included in the Chadwyck-Healey *Early English Books Online* and Gale/Cengage *Eighteenth-Century Collections Online* databases, and are also available in print-on-demand paperback editions. Many of the notes of the early (and later) commentators are usefully collected in Earl Miner (ed.), *Paradise Lost, 1668–1968: Three Centuries of Commentary* (Lewisburg, 2004). The most admired modern edition of *Paradise Lost* is that of Alastair Fowler in the Longman Annotated English Poets series (2nd edition, London, 1998). This, indeed, contains a mine of invaluable material in its Introduction and notes, but its very dense annotation (often occupying more space on the page than the poem itself, and frequently referring the reader to other secondary material) perhaps makes it more suitable for advanced students than for those approaching the poem for the first time.

Biography and Reference

An excellent brief biography of Milton by Gordon Campbell is included in the *Oxford Dictionary of National Biography*, and has been reprinted separately as a small book in Oxford University Press's 'Very Important People' series (2007). Campbell has also compiled a *Milton Chronology* (Basingstoke, 1997) which gives full details of Milton's life and writings, year by year. Perhaps the most generally useful full-length modern biography is Barbara K. Lewalski's *The Life of John Milton* (Oxford, 2000, revised 2003). The early biographies, collected by Helen Darbishire as *The Early Lives of Milton* (London, 1932), contain many fascinating insights into Milton's life and work by his immediate contemporaries and successors. Milton's presentations of himself in his work are anthologized by John S. Diekhoff in *Milton on Himself* (2nd edition, London, 1965) and expertly discussed by Stephen M. Fallon in *Milton's Peculiar Grace: Self-representation and Authority* (Ithaca, 2007) and in 'Milton on Himself' in *Milton in Context* (see below).

Reference entries on virtually every aspect of Milton's career and works are provided in William B. Hunter *et al.*, *A Milton Encyclopedia*, 9 vols. (Lewisburg, 1978–83) and Thomas N. Corns, *The Milton Encyclopedia* (New Haven, 2012). Useful information on many aspects of Milton's life and writing is also to be found in Stephen B. Dobranski (ed.), *Milton in Context* (Cambridge, 2010).

Criticism

Four collections of essays provide a useful conspectus of current views on *Paradise Lost*. These are: Dennis Danielson (ed.), *The Cambridge Companion to Milton* (2nd edition, 1999); Thomas Corns (ed.), *A Companion to Milton* (Oxford, 2001); Nicholas McDowell and Nigel Smith (eds), *The Oxford Handbook of Milton* (Oxford, 2009); Paul Hammond and Blair Worden (eds), *John Milton: Life, Writing, Reputation* (Oxford, 2010).

For reasons suggested in the present book, some of the best Milton criticism is some of the earliest. Milton criticism between 1628 and 1811 is conveniently collected in the two volumes devoted to Milton in the Routledge *Critical Heritage* series (ed. John T. Shawcross, London, 1970, 1972). Worthy of particular attention are the prefatory poem by Marvell, the comments of Voltaire in his *Essay on Epic Poetry*, the *Spectator* papers by Joseph Addison, and Samuel Johnson's *Rambler* papers on Milton's style, and 'Life of Milton' in his *Lives of the Poets*. Early nineteenth-century criticism is usefully collected in Joseph A. Wittreich (ed.), *The Romantics on Milton* (Cleveland, 1970). Coleridge's often brilliant remarks on *Paradise Lost* are also available in *Coleridge on the Seventeenth Century*, ed. R. F. Brinkley (Durham NC, 1955).

Of the many modern introductory studies of *Paradise Lost*, probably the most useful and accessible is that by David Loewenstein in the Cambridge University Press *Landmarks of World Literature* series (Cambridge, 1993). G. K. Hunter's volume in the Unwin *Critical Studies* series (London, 1980) also contains many valuable insights. Charles Martindale's 'Writing Epic: *Paradise Lost*' (in *The Oxford Handbook of Milton*: see above) provides an excellent essay-length introduction to Milton's epic ambitions.

The liveliest modern treatment of Milton's style in *Paradise Lost* remains Christopher Ricks's *Milton's Grand Style* (Oxford, 1963), which makes full and telling use of the eighteenth-century commentators. The effect of foreign (particular classical) languages on Milton is expertly described by John K. Hale in *Milton's Languages* (Cambridge, 1997). The verse-rhythms of *Paradise Lost* are illuminatingly discussed by John Creaser in his essay in *The Oxford Handbook of Milton* (see above). The poetic resonances of Milton's treatment of the Fall are examined in Paul Hammond's essay in *John Milton: Life, Writing, Reputation* (see above). The relationship between narrator and narrative in *Paradise Lost* is explored by Fred Parker in 'Marvell on Milton: Why the Poem Rhymes Not', *Cambridge Quarterly*, 20 (1991), 183–209.

Milton's relation to his biblical sources is now most fully documented in Matthew Stallard (ed.), *Paradise Lost: The Biblically Annotated Edition* (Macon, 2011). Milton's use of the classics is expertly discussed by Charles Martindale in *John Milton and the Transformation of Classical Epic* (London, 1986) and in 'Milton's Classicism' (in Volume 3 of *The Oxford History of Classical Reception in English Literature*, ed. David Hopkins and Charles Martindale (Oxford, 2012)). On this subject, see also Colin Burrow in *Epic Romance: Homer to Milton* (Oxford, 1993), David Hopkins's chapter on 'Milton and the Classics' in *John Milton: Life, Writing, Reputation* (see above), and Maggie Kilgour, *Milton and the Metamorphosis of Ovid* (Oxford, 2012).

Milton's theological beliefs are explored by Dennis R. Danielson, in *Milton's Good God: A Study in Literary Theodicy* (Cambridge, 1982), and by William Poole, in *Milton and the Idea of the Fall* (Cambridge, 2005). The background and authorship of his treatise on Christian theology is examined by Gordon Campbell, Thomas N. Corns, John K. Hale, and Fiona J. Tweedie, in *Milton and the Manuscript of* De Doctrina Christiana (Oxford, 2007).

The figure of Satan receives central treatment in most critical accounts of *Paradise Lost*. Particularly illuminating commentary on the political dimension of Milton's portrayal is to be found in Blair Worden's 'Milton's Republicanism and the Tyranny of Heaven', in *Machiavelli and Republicanism*, ed. Gisela Bock, Quentin Skinner, and Maurizio Viroli (Cambridge, 1990), pp. 225–45. In *The Devil as Muse* (Waco, 2011), Fred Parker offers some challenging reflections on Milton's depiction of Satan in relation to questions of poetic inspiration.

Defences of Milton against charges of misogyny in his depiction of Eve are presented by Barbara K. Lewalski in 'Milton on Women – Yet Again', in *Problems for Feminist Criticism*, ed. Sally Minogue (London, 1990), pp. 46–69, and by Diane Kelsey McColley in *Milton's Eve* (Urbana, 1983), and in her contribution to *The Cambridge Companion to Milton* (see above). For a variety of recent views on this topic, see also Catherine Gimelli Martin (ed.), *Milton and Gender* (Cambridge, 2004).

Milton's depictions of Adam and Eve's life in Paradise are sensitively discussed by A. J. Smith in *The Metaphysics of Love* (Cambridge, 1985) (pp. 14–28, 114–45, 323–7). The dynamic potential of Eden is helpfully expounded by Barbara K. Lewalski in 'Innocence and Experience in Milton's Eden', in *New Essays on* Paradise Lost, ed. Thomas Kranidas (Berkeley, LA and London, 1971), pp. 86–117. Milton's depiction of Adam and Eve's marriage and its background is also explored in James Grantham Turner, *One Flesh: Paradisal Marriage and Sexual Relations in the Age of Milton* (Oxford, 1987).

Good starting points for considering the political dimension of *Paradise Lost* are Martin Dzelzainis's essay in *The Oxford Handbook to Milton* (see above), David Norbrook's chapter in his *Writing the English Republic* (Cambridge, 1999), and Blair Worden's 'Milton's Republicanism and the Tyranny of Heaven' (see above). See also Mary Ann Radzinowicz, 'The Politics of *Paradise Lost*', in *Politics of Discourse: The Literature and History of Seventeenth-Century England*, ed. Kevin Sharpe and Steven N. Zwicker (Berkeley, LA and London, 1987), pp. 204–29; Sharon Achenstein, *Milton and the Revolutionary Reader* (Princeton, 1994).

Milton's influence and later reputation are discussed by Dustin Griffin, in *Regaining Paradise: Milton and the Eighteenth Century*

(Cambridge, 1986), Christine Rees, in *Johnson's Milton* (Cambridge, 2010), Lucy Newlyn, in *Paradise Lost and the Romantic Reader* (Oxford, 1993), and Erik Gray, in *Milton and the Victorians* (Ithaca, 2009); and in the essays by Nicholas Von Maltzahn in *The Cambridge Companion to Milton*, by Kay Gilliland Stevenson in *A Companion to Milton*, and by David Fairer and Tom Lockwood in *John Milton: Life, Writing, Reputation*.

Milton's illustrators and his influence on the visual arts are discussed in Marcia R. Pointon, *Milton and English Art* (Manchester, 1970), and in Robert Woof, Howard J. M. Hanley and Stephen Hebron, Paradise Lost: *The Poem and its Illustrators* (Grasmere, 2004).

Index to lines and passages from *Paradise Lost*

Reading Paradise Lost, First Edition. David Hopkins.
© 2013 John Wiley & Sons, Ltd. Published 2013 by John Wiley & Sons, Ltd.

Index to main text and notes